# Wandering Souls

'And I will hide my face from them, and they shall be devoured' (Deuteronomy 21: 17): for, when man is deprived of Divine protection he is exposed to all dangers, and becomes the butt of all fortuitous circumstances: his fortune and misfortune then depend on chance. Alas! how terrible a threat!

Maimonides, 1190

# Wandering Souls

Tobie Nathan

Translated by Stephen Muecke

polity

First published in French as *Les Âmes errantes* © L'Iconoclaste, Paris, 2017

This English edition © Polity Press, 2019

Polity Press
65 Bridge Street
Cambridge CB2 1UR, UK

Polity Press
101 Station Landing
Suite 300
Medford, MA 02155, USA

ISBN-13: 978-1-5095-3495-1 (hardback)
ISBN-13: 978-1-5095-3496-8 (paperback)

A catalogue record for this book is available from the British Library.

Library of Congress Cataloging-in-Publication Data
Names: Nathan, Tobie, author.
Title: Wandering souls / Tobie Nathan.
Other titles: Ames errantes. English
Description: Cambridge, UK : Polity Press, 2019. | Includes bibliographical references and index.
Identifiers: LCCN 2019009981 (print) | LCCN 2019012902 (ebook) | ISBN 9781509534975 (Epub) | ISBN 9781509534951 | ISBN 9781509534951(hardback) | ISBN 9781509534968(pbk.)
Subjects: LCSH: Muslim youth--France--Attitudes. | Muslim youth--France--Social conditions. | Islamic fundamentalism--France. | Youth--Psychology. | Radicalization--France. | Radicalism--Psychological aspects. | Radicalism--Religious aspects--Islam. | Youth--France--Social conditions--21st century.
Classification: LCC DC34.5.M87 (ebook) | LCC DC34.5.M87 N3813 2019 (print) | DDC 305.235088/2970944--dc23
LC record available at https://lccn.loc.gov/2019009981

Typeset in 11 on 14 pt Sabon by
Servis Filmsetting Ltd, Stockport, Cheshire
Printed and bound in Great Britain by CPI Group (UK) Ltd, Croydon

Cet ouvrage publié dans le cadre du programme d'aide à la publication bénéficie du soutien du Ministère des Affaires Etrangères et du Service Culturel de l'Ambassade de France représenté aux Etats-Unis.

This work received support from the French Ministry of Foreign Affairs and the Cultural Services of the French Embassy in the United States through their publishing assistance program.

The publisher has used its best endeavours to ensure that the URLs for external websites referred to in this book are correct and active at the time of going to press. However, the publisher has no responsibility for the websites and can make no guarantee that a site will remain live or that the content is or will remain appropriate.

Every effort has been made to trace all copyright holders, but if any have been overlooked the publisher will be pleased to include any necessary credits in any subsequent reprint or edition.

For further information on Polity, visit our website:
politybooks.com

# Contents

# *Acknowledgements*

To the Interministerial Committee for the Prevention of Delinquency and Radicalisation, whose support enabled the clinical work to take place among the young people and their families, I offer thanks.

To my friends: Catherine, indefatigable guide, eternal accomplice; to Nathalie, delightful, spurring me on with indefinite, open questions; to Jean-Luc, who never misses a passing soul; to Mustapha, lighting these dark times; to Amélie, with the larger picture in mind; to Anthony, free explorer of possibilities; to Marie-Anne, ancestor in a child's body; and to Thierry, finally, who has the carefulness of an angel . . . to each, my admiration.

# Prologue

Stranger, though a still poorer man should come here, it would not be right for me to insult him, for all strangers and beggars are from Jove.

Homer, *The Odyssey*, Book 14

1958. First winter in Paris. We didn't really know what the word 'winter' meant. The cold chilled us to the bone, penetrated our lungs, cracked the footpaths and tingled our reddened ears. I was ten. We came from Cairo, in Egypt, and had spent some time in Rome. In countries like Italy houses are refuges from the baking heat of the streets. As soon as we arrived in France, it was the opposite! It was cold outside and sometimes hot inside. We hadn't been introduced to scarves, woollen balaclavas, socks inside boots or two pairs of gloves. The delight in blowing out clouds of steam, like bison breath, the happy squeaking of shoes on fresh powdery snow, or even better, jumping with both feet into the frozen gutters. Gennevilliers! We approached the town with circumspection, like frightened animals whose cages had been taken away.

*Prologue*

Our first port of call, before Gennevilliers, had been the 9th *arrondissement* in Paris, Faubourg-Montmartre; greyness, maids' rooms and seedy hotels. We had arrived in a Paris that was cold and wet, where classrooms, canteens and clinics were overheated. The result quickly followed. Infection. Mycobacterium tuberculosis must have been xenophobic, preferring immigrant kids; the awful smell of antibiotic sprays, forever imprinted in the nostrils! But at least Paris was anonymous. For me, the indifference of people in the street was a sign of freedom. If I am 'nobody', then nobody will recognise me. I enjoyed slipping between the passers-by with the mad hope of becoming an everyman, being 'integrated'. One day, I thought without conviction, we'll be hitting the streets just like them, invisible and satisfied, content as fish in a bowl.

So, these were the happy suburbs with their housing estates. At least there the adults didn't pay much attention to the children's lives! Our adolescent Sundays were spent roaming around Paris. But, coming back down the Avenue de Clichy with my mates, crossing those little streets that snaked off somewhere or other, among stray dogs, dubious shops, old ladies on the prowl, we felt the weight of those glances and the inevitable insults were thrown. Once we got to the periphery, Porte de Clichy, we boarded the 139, a bus with the rear platform – the good old TN6 model, the very ones that were requisitioned for the Vél d'Hiv round-up[1] – in an atmosphere that was oozing sweat. Bouncing around on the hard wooden benches, we recognised the conductor, the workers from the Chausson or Hispano factories, the drunk from the *Brazza* café. They certainly recognised us. Everyone in Gennevilliers knew us! We were the children from the Claude-Debussy Estate. The Jews, the refugees.

At that time there were not many refugees. Afterwards, many more came, and from everywhere. Millions of them! Before the war there were Italians, of course, Poles and Spaniards, then Jews from the East, Germany and Poland; and even earlier, at the beginning of the twentieth century, Russians. They were not forgotten, but they were no longer the immediate focus of abuse and hatred, having been replaced by 'Arabs', who were most often Kabyles. At that time, Algerians were not refugees – Algeria was supposed to be French – but 'relocated workers'. In 1958, we Egyptian Jews were among the first refugees since the war.

As one would expect, the language of the immigrants generated local slang, especially when it came to what to call them. They were called 'bicots' because many had 'Larbi', meaning 'the Arab' as a first name. 'Larbi' became 'Larbicot', after 'l'abricot' [apricot] because of their sometimes coppery skin-colour. Larbicot . . . *bicot*. It was an insult, yet it was simple derivation from the word for Arab. They were belittled by being called 'crouillats', which sounded a bit like 'couille' [testicle] or 'couillon' [dickhead], but it was in fact a deformation of the Arab *akhouya*, 'my brother', an affectionate greeting often used by Algerian immigrants. As for us kids, these 'Arabs' certainly weren't our 'brothers', but co-pupils at the local school, and often our friends.

We got our share. They called us 'youpin', 'youde' or 'youtre', insults also deriving from the way Jews designated themselves. *Yehoudi*, in Hebrew, simply meant 'Jew', that is, 'of the Judah tribe'. Just like *bicot* or *crouillat*, these insults are a label. It is easy to decode the meaning: 'No use trying to hide or melt into the population at large. I know all about you, even the way you talk about yourself in your own language: "crouillat", "youde", "polack" . . . I know you so well that I can twist your own words into mockery.' As the Latin proverb has it, 'if you know his name, you capture the person'.

These were the insults of future slave-drivers! At the time, no one cared how the labelled reacted to their labelling. Would it occur to anti-Semites that sometimes Jews might end up believing a little in the image reflected back to them? Up until they extricate themselves from that image, always a violent process.

The Claude-Debussy Estate where we had landed was surrounded by the dead. When I exited the ground floor of Building G, there were dead on my left, real ones, in the large cemetery of rue du Puits-Guyon. On the right, the slum, the social death sentence for North African immigrants. And opposite was an automobile cemetery, a gigantic car junkyard that we called 'the scrap'. It was owned by Gypsies and was guarded by two big black hounds and a German Shepherd. And when we dreamt, eyes closed, at the wheel of an old rusty Cadillac, they would come and drive us out, their fangs bared. Especially the big male; we called him Baskerville . . .

The housing estate was still bogged down in the mud of the construction sites and had scarcely emerged from the ground. It just happened that the construction of this set of buildings with its whiff of Le Corbusier (splashes of primary colours; cobalt blue, lemon yellow, and carmen red on brutalist cement), coincided with our inopportune arrival in France, expelled from Egypt after the Suez crisis, and dumped there, blown by the wind, in Claude-Debussy city estate, a 'radiant' city.[2] We were the 'glorious' ones, not because this decrepit architecture might have inspired us, but because we rode the waves of friendly competition. Of the hundred and fifty families who lived there for a time, the Egyptian Jews made up a good third, maybe more. In our little ghetto, we could speak the old languages, keep our customs going for a while, and we could laugh about them, and about those of the others, whom we simply thought of as 'French'. We could evoke our lost land as we made fun of our parents' and grand-parents' accents. We were carefree, fun-loving, high-spirited. We spread out from there before too long; left home to blend into society, in one place or another, high or low. I often think that those years spent in our little community, due to the haphazard siting of the buildings, allowed us a soft landing, a less traumatic arrival than that of many others whom I rubbed shoulders with later. These were the benefits of a communal airlock, so far from the caricatures with which 'communitarianism' (said with a grimace, of course) is dressed up.

2015. Winters are milder than in the old days. House-call to rue Chandon, a street that intersects with the one I lived in as a child. I know that in the Claude-Debussy Estate that I'm looking at today, one last Jewish family is left, abandoned there because of setbacks and bad luck. The grandparents and parents live each day in fear. The letterbox is covered with anti-Semitic abuse. Today the death-threats come not from the whims of some blue-eyed field marshal,[3] but from the followers of a gloomy Mesopotamian caliph. I scarcely recognise the place. Where the cemetery was, is a glorious new Estate, and where the scrapyard was, yet another glorious Estate. As for the slum, on its soil fertilised by tears and sweat, any number of other glorious Estates have grown, infinite expanses of cement under a stone sky. In the rue Claude-Debussy, nearly empty in the early afternoon, a completely veiled woman battles against the wind as she drags a little girl along by the hand. It brings me to a standstill. The scene reminds me of a photo of De Gaulle and his wife in 1969, after the referendum, battling the wind on an Irish beach. The end of a world. I have a strange feeling, a mixture of anxiety and vertigo. A feeling of *déjà-vu*, no doubt. I see this Estate so often in my dreams. It is true I lived in it. Here, my soul pulsed with feelings. I experienced my first transports of knowledge. I covered every nook and cranny, then I forgot it. And I began to see it in my dreams. It courses in my veins, and yet it resists my conscious mind. The uneasiness I feel in coming here again after fifty-odd years is evidence (I'm not fooling myself) of a visceral attachment to the place. But doubt is stronger. I know that once I turn my gaze away, I will forget again. The certainty of the world falters, as if the intensity of my memories had made the real seem strange.

When we got to Gennevilliers, Claude-Debussy Estate, we came from a long way away, from a Middle East that had started to go up in flames; from a torpid land of gods where mythology was entwined with everyday life. Over there Moses was a relative and the Pharaoh a neighbour. Another mythology governed France. We were surprised (enchanted!) by a phrase that we kept hearing, even in the mouths of babes, to lay claim to their freedom of speech: 'We are in a Republic!' Before long we were claiming it in turn, and even more often, intoxicated just by the promise of this freedom. We kids were very quick to adapt, straddling thousands of kilometres and historical millennia with our giant strides. We were ignorant of the fact that the emptiness we thought we had overcome in a matter of months would never disappear; it would remain in us, as both a void of unresolved anxieties, and an energy for future passions. The problem for migrant children is not, as they used to think, the difficulty of adapting, but is in their excessive impressionability. At the time, nothing is visible, but the abyss deepens secretly, and erupts a dozen years later as a bundle of negativities. If a rule had to be made about this, I would put it like this:

> If migrants are particularly susceptible to emergent ideologies, it is because these ideologies come to fill a void left in them by feelings with no material basis.

There are words from far away, coming from the languages of my childhood, that impact on words here, inflating their meaning. *Canif* [penknife], for example, which means 'latrines' in Egyptian Arabic. I avoid using this word in French, no doubt out of a worry of slipping into another language without noticing. Or worse, the word *kassar* that totally coincidentally means 'casser' [break], linking synonymy and homonymy. I avoid that one too. Instead, 'when I need to say *break*', I use 'briser' or 'rompre' or whatever. There are words that make the borders between worlds uncertain. I am not alone in fearing certain words and avoiding them like the plague. First and second generation migrant children in France have the experience, deep within them, of a fundamental lack of fit between the word and the thing. What they retain is a fount of rage. They want to pick a fight both with their past (their origins) and with their future (the world that is promised them). They are eager for a new world, a world that is waiting for them, a world that will resolve opposites and harmonise disparities. They will join the first revolution that comes along. They will be proselytisers for the latest ideas, thinking that in one fell swoop they can wipe out their distant allegiances and the gap that separates them from their neighbours. That was me! On the barricades in May '68, screaming out a communard song, I was no longer Jewish, or Egyptian, or foreign, I was part of that growing ferment, that breaking wave; I was at the avant-garde of a unified humanity. That, too, was Gennevilliers, a city of communists and workers, one of the gateways of France, interspersed with the rejects and overflow of societies that were breaking down, a gateway in France, like Saint-Denis, Aubervilliers or Belleville and so many others across the country.

Since then these gateways have become blocked, or sometimes occupied, and no longer allow free passage to a society that carries on regardless. The Luth quarter of Gennevilliers no longer has buses going into it for fear of stoning; its main mosque used to be attended by the Kouachi brothers, responsible for the 7 January 2015 attacks, a mosque they left because they found it too moderate; Gennevilliers with its sleeper cells hatching plots for simultaneous attacks planned for the four corners of francophone Europe; Marseilles, Paris, Lyon and Brussels. My beloved Gennevilliers!

I wanted to approach these 'radicalised' young people, these children from the same streets who came after me, from the concrete stoops of the same buildings, and who I feel resemble me. Migrants, like me; estate kids, just like me ... Radicalised? Why not say 'radicals'? 'To be a radical', wrote Marx, 'is to grasp things by the root.'[4] If there is any dominant characteristic that they have, then it is their willingness to overturn what is taken for granted, turn questions around by refusing our premises, to no longer accept the principles or forms of knowledge with which they grew up. No doubt they are radical, but not in Marx's way, who added, 'But for man the root is man himself.' Because for them, the root is not man, but God, and not just any god, but Allah! I'm taken aback: how can they think like that? But I immediately reconsider: thinking is not 'thinking the same thing as me'!

I certainly wanted to touch the hearts of these kids, today's 'radicals', but mostly I wanted to appeal to their minds, through thinking. I wanted to come up with ideas and concepts that make their issues less impenetrable to our minds.

I have been working for decades with migrant populations. Time and again I have tried to draw attention to the madness of considering them in their nakedness, as if they came from nowhere, as if they didn't belong to anyone, treating them like orphans without gods or myths.[5] This is why I put together clinical arrangements where their languages are respected, as well as those of their parents and ancestors; arrangements that make use of the resources of their own worlds.[6] While the concepts that I present here come, for the most part, from this type of clinical work, I want to extend the discussion beyond that to introduce a way of coming to terms with a social phenomenon that is also a political movement with international ramifications. It is no longer a matter of isolated phenomena, cases seen as clinical or social. I am not talking about data, but about masses, weighty issues, strange kinds of attraction.

The problem of radical Islamic youth has not only invaded the media, but it has anaesthetised our brains, obsessed us all day long and trashed our ideals. Right now might be a good time to reassess how much we need to change our thinking, our theories and our modes of action. The things that have happened have unhinged and maddened us – the attacks of course, but also the way alterity is obviously very close, brushing past us, shouting at us every day. And we are still driven mad by what's happened, or in shock, still invaded by alterity.

I am writing about what I heard, felt, perceived and conceived, on meeting them, in exchanges with their loved-ones, in reading the dozens of books that are dedicated to them every month. Perhaps you will be surprised not to find any 'psychological profiles' here (as if they mean anything), or any statistics. Apart from the fact that I'm against numbers as an easy way out, always deflecting phenomena towards the most banal ideas (the mediocrity of averages), I would like to come to terms with what their fate has in store for them, and get a good fix on the forces running through them. I want to understand the dynamics of how, over a period of a few weeks or months, the ignorance of a hash-smoking delinquent from the estates turns into the expertise of a Hadith philosopher; or how a naive young girl, stylish and from a nice area, becomes a warrior in a burqa looking for a husband with a Kalashnikov; or how the innocence of a young high-school nerd turns into the commitment of a jihadist off to fight in the combat zones in Syria. The history of radicalisations is not that of 'natures'. It consists of metamorphoses, moments of immobility, then sudden intoxication at the thought of other futures.[7] So it is an often unpredictable history. Nor should one freeze the moment a word is dropped during a police interrogation, or during an investigation by a sociologist or journalist, or even a psychiatric consultation, but rather enable oneself to imagine how people change.

This movement can only be rendered in sequences. Each chapter is a pause, with enough time for reflection. We can take our breath and then start off again trying not to lose anything of a subject which, we sense, eludes each word and each sigh. I needed these stationary moments spent in conceptual analysis in order to reconstruct the flow of these actual destinies. At the end of the journey, I hope that the patient reader will be rewarded by some kind of form emerging from the fog.

This text is based on clinical material gleaned in the context of a preventive setting aimed, by intervening early on, at avoiding any slippage towards violent action. The young people who have benefited, for the most part, were not 'sick' and were never seeking help. Their thoughts and behaviour are no doubt extreme enough without having to deal with real violence (at the front line in battle, the horror of the massacre of innocents, decapitations, rapes). I am certain that some people whom I didn't meet, returning from Syria, or people who committed attacks here in France, even if they were driven by the same ideology, were massively changed by what they did. It is true that in every single case, whether it is that of an ideologue or an activist, we should never give up trying to understand things, events and people, but assassins should still be subject to uncompromising judicial treatment.

## Prologue

Understanding is a prayer addressed to reality. It should be broad enough to accommodate the expanse of our perception. But understanding in no way means excusing. The victims, the victims' families, the environment – in short, 'society' – remain in the grip of events. They demand reparation. The intelligence that one brings to bear to understand the facts is part and parcel of the reparation. And justice even more so.

I have called this book *Wandering Souls*. As a guide for the authorities and for humanists, it is meant to calm emotions and to help see them more clearly at meetings with these children who imagine they are ancestors or prophets. But it is also a guide for these same wandering children, with captured souls, in thrall to harmful forces, to maybe help them find a way home one day.

# 1
# *Secularity and the War of the Gods*

Many old gods ascend from their graves; they are disenchanted and hence take the form of impersonal forces. They
strive to gain power over our lives and again they resume
their eternal struggle with one another. What is hard for
modern man, and especially for the younger generation, is
to measure up to workaday existence.[1]

Max Weber, *Science as a Vocation*

We were children, just boys! Our games were often
fights; arguments could escalate into insults. We knew
that words attacking family, race or religion were the
last words before the first punch. And when a mediator,
a teacher or teacher's assistant, tried to reason with us,
he would call upon the law: 'You don't have the right to
call him a dirty Jew . . .' he would remind us. 'Why?' the
other would protest, 'we are in a Republic!' At the time,
the Republic was all about rights, not constraints. It
didn't forbid, it authorised; it didn't hinder, it unleashed.
It's true we ventured to the limits of these rights, pushing
our educators to their last line of defence. Nevertheless,

it was still the case that we perceived 'the Republic' (we wouldn't be able to give a definition of this entity) as a kind of divinity that put rich and poor, strong and weak, boss and subject, teacher and pupil, on the same footing. Childish naivety . . . but also candour in a time of opportunities.

I was terrified of school – even to this day. I had a visceral sense of its desire to destroy our modes of belonging, to make a mockery of them. There was a simple principle: after being subject to a series of critiques, gibes, making fun, one inevitably felt all alone in one's Jewishness, Arabness, probably even in one's 'Auvergeness' (should one be from that province), and yearning to come and melt into the common mass of 'secularity' [*laïcité*]. So, we kept our singularity to ourselves, even if it was pretty obvious. We pretended. We even developed critical responses, as in 'reaction formations'. We made ourselves out to be more French than the French, more secular than the secular. At the time we didn't use the word *laïcité*, that came later . . .

Today, it is repeated over and over, as if its meaning were clear. And yet it is an ambiguous word; if you analyse it, you find a few unexpected meanings.

The French word *laïc* comes from the Greek, *laos* which means people. If you refer to its etymology, *laïc* goes back to 'popular', and therefore to 'common'. The meaning is not too far from the word 'vulgar', which in turn derives from a Latin root, *vulgus*, the 'crowd' or the 'multitude'.[2] 'Vulgar' has remained close to its root, still designating that which is of the greatest number and which, in consequence, is 'primary'. 'Laïc', being more scholarly, took a more specific meaning in its opposition to 'cleric'. Apparently in the Middle Ages, 'laïc' signified 'ignorant', without religious instruction, the contrary of the *cleric*, who was a lettered man, supposedly knowing the scriptures. By keeping this first distinction in mind – laïc as 'ignorant' opposed to cleric as 'initiated' – we will see that it has not entirely disappeared!

Following the religious wars that devastated France in the sixteenth century, the word took on other meanings. 'Laïc' came to designate an institutional reality. The word did not imply that all French people should be laïc (ignorant of the religious), but that the State, the law of the land, philosophy and above all teaching should be freed of all religious influence. This meaning, that made 'laïc' an adjective that could be applied to organisations, is today contradicted (even though it is fairly robust) by semantic shifts running through society on the move . . .

At the beginning of the twentieth century, at the height of the Third Republic, the State succeeded for the first time in unifying the country and normalising souls by putting in place obligatory and secular[3] public schooling. In the space of a generation, the country saw the disappearance of regional languages,[4] and a great number of the pagan rituals that have still survived in the countryside[5] as cults associated with springs or wells or death rituals. The Republic came to impose a more aggressive connotation on the word 'laïc', which got closer and closer to 'anticlerical'. Henceforth, a *laïc* is not just someone ignorant in religious matters, no longer simply actively supporting the independence of the institutions of the State, liberated from the tutelage of the Church, but he begins to be a priest-hater. After Rabelais, he will sometimes be defined as a *papefigue*,[6] or a *prêtrophobe,* a sixteenth-century term meaning a man with a 'phobia' of priests. 'Prêtrophobe' . . . We are not far from certain terms that appear today when people are being critical of a widespread attitude, as in 'homophobe' or 'islamophobe'.

In addition, there is an implicit notion that attaches itself to this secularity without speakers being aware of it, a sort of double unconscious emerging like that enhanced violence of the long repressed. If the State, having fought savagely, as we know, against heretics, Cathars, Jews and witches until the last moments of the Inquisition, then devastated whole regions to eradicate Calvinists and Protestants; if, having swept through the countryside during the Terror, beheading, drowning and burning people, animals and crops in order to annihilate nobles and ecclesiasticals; if, after all that, the State still needed to legislate and impose peace on society through the much-touted 'separation of Church and State', it is because the forces involved, those that have so often nearly broken up the State, cannot be mastered. In a sense, the 1905 law on secularism flows from a never-ending failure: the Republic cannot – will not – allow these forces to express themselves. They are no doubt too primitive, too archaic. The Republic cannot allow itself to let them blossom, to seize institutions and agencies. All it can do is forbid them from entering the spheres of power.

But these forces have a name. We have always known them: *they are the gods* – not religions, but gods! They are the true protagonists. And I mean all the gods, the pagan deities as much as the monotheistic gods, each with its specific requirements, from the Catholic God to the Protestant, Islamic, or Jewish ones. And we must agree that the 1905 law not only signed off on the failure of the Republic, but also the failure of religions. This law acknowledged the fact that there was no credibility in the promises that religions made about knowing their gods and keeping their moods in check and, in the process, protecting people from their violence and bloodthirstiness. All these religions had failed in their attempts to master their gods.

So, what has remained hidden behind the notion of secularity, ever since the first years of the twentieth century, is its negative, what it has built a bulwark against the uncontrollable violence of the gods. And it is these same gods that are reappearing today, and they have become even more cruel to the extent that they are in direct competition with one another because of globalisation and the accelerated movement of populations.

*This war – that has been put on hold, that has taken place many times before and is just waiting to break out again – has to be given its proper name: the 'war of the gods'.* So, when the politicians announce that 'we are at war' without even having declared war on anyone; when we meet young people ready to pick a fight, mindlessly looking for some battle-ground, it is actually this unnamed war that is driving them.[7]

While they look like they are running away from secularity, my calculation is that these young radicalised people are reactivating to its opposite, its grimacing double. It is no good trying to reason with them by reminding them of the values of the Republic, as if they hadn't understood them, or had forgotten them. To the contrary, they live them through and through, right down to discovering their foundations and reviving the conditions that created them. They want to be initiated into this hidden part of our world, this *war of the gods* from which our society has tried to protect itself, precisely through secularity, and which their engagement brings out in the open again.

Addressing the problem in terms of people and their individual motivations, difficulties they might have had in their childhood or adolescence, and ignoring the forces that are attached to them, and which according to their own testimony, *possess them*, is an intellectual error, a bad way of approaching the question. Worse, it is lazy.

When a young man of twenty-five confronts the combined forces of the police and the security forces, offering his breast to their bullets as he yells *Allahou Akbar* ('Allah is *the* greatest'), he inscribes a surplus of divine existence into the world. Let's call things by their names. The terror we feel is of a mythological order. In this sequence of events, the death of a man who in full awareness sacrifices himself, reinforces the existence of his god,[8] according to a reverse accounting: one man less, a bit more divinity. This has nothing to do with suicide or the promise of eternal life; it is all about an unstoppable religious logic: the transmutation of human lives into divine power.

We are surrounded by these forces – these gods – that have taken hold of these young people, that have captured them, and put them to work. Whatever our reaction is, they still concern us. Sooner or later our existence, our lives, will be equally in question – if not as victims, then at least as political witnesses. The pressure will be on, not only to rethink our institutions, but also our mode of existence in the world.

Of course, these forces are also apparent in a more concrete fashion, as actual groupings made up of activists, fighters – older, seasoned, more active – also recruiters, targeting individual vulnerabilities, carrying out *actual kidnapping of souls*, and political activists with *revolutionary style strategies*, such as the destabilisation of social spaces and the seizure of power. It is appropriate to respond to these groups on the same terrain that they engage us: politics. But political action does not preclude the knowledge of gods, nor the analysis of the strategies of those possessed by God.

Once action and its associated fuss has passed, when the alarms are going off in every quarter, when our actions have devolved into reactions, then it is time for reflexion. And then the burning question arises, one that is all the more compelling because it remains unasked; *what if laicity were no longer able to guard against the war of the gods?* Do we have an alternative solution?[9]

When I look at how the people in charge deal with this – politicians, experts, journalists – I am amazed. They oscillate between two attitudes, only two! Firstly, they are compassionate and understanding about the individual problems that they think might have driven these young people to such extremes, including towards a kind of suicide. Secondly, they have recourse to the law, the Republic and laicity. In the first case psychological and social work programmes are the prescription (more listening, more services, more retraining); in the second they recommend the rigorous application of law and order (more police, more repressive laws, more sanctions). But both compassion and reliance on the law are equally ineffective – we see it every day.

Compassion is insulting. Those on the receiving end always see it as an attempt to ensnare them. A line from Sartre in *The Devil and the Good Lord* does a better job than a long explanation:

To him who gives you a kiss or a blow,
You should render a kiss or a blow;
But to him who gives what you cannot render,
Offer all the hatred within your hearts.
For you were slaves, and he enslaved you;
You were humiliated, and he increased your humiliation.[10]

Inevitably compassion without reciprocity unleashes
rebellion. This is a common-sense lesson that should be
remembered every time someone is taken into care or
custody.

And if recourse to the law often seems to fail to
engage, this is certainly not because the radicalised are
lawless – they recognise another law! I will never forget
the beaming smile of the young man detained for par-
ticipation in a terrorist network, the defiance deep in his
eyes, and him declaring, 'Do you really think that prison
will make me any less determined?'

The denial of our law is a declaration of fidelity to
another law. Still, we can derive an aphorism from
this: *the refusal of the law is always a profession of
faith*. We, coming from a supposed 'Christian tradition'
should know this. One just has to delve into the origins
of Christianity and look at what happened to the first
martyrs who, in affirming their faith, came up against
Roman law.

As for the judicial treatment of the problem, it might
well begin interestingly enough through the way the
trial is brought out open into the public, but once the
verdict is handed down it all unravels. We all know that
in prison values are reversed: outlaws become heroes,
criminal actions are kinds of medals, and laicity a religious necessity.

I must say that I prefer another way of framing the question of radicalisation. Not compassion or recourse to the law, but a rigorous investigation of the forces present, their nature, their names, their modes of existence, the ways in which they capture people, the demands they place upon them ... Forty-five years of clinical practice with migrants has taught me a rule: always be on side with the way the other understands their forces and resources; never their failings, disorders or what they lack. In the case of radicalised young people, we first have to note the intelligence of the beings and forces, evaluate the power of what is at stake and above all: produce thinking.

Consequently, these furious, captive young people, who have revealed the foundations of laicity to us, will have the status they attribute to themselves taken seriously: they are proselytisers for a divinity that does not hide its intention to steal people's minds.

# 2

# *The Veil as Membrane*

And every woman who prays or prophesies with her head uncovered dishonours her head, for it is just as if her head were shaved. If a woman does not cover her head, let her hair be cut off. And if it is shameful for a woman to have her hair cut or shaved off, she should cover her head.

Paul, Corinthians 11: 5–6

She was born in Paris. Her parents are both Senegalese emigrants. They are not really *im*migrants because their French is not good; they live in terror of institutions; they are travel weary and perpetually nostalgic. She covers herself completely in swathes of black. Even in the height of summer she wears woollen gloves, black as well. Only her eyes and the bridge of her nose can be seen; two huge eyes outlined with kohl. She has a frank, open and curious gaze, and yet she moves like a dancer with a proud carriage, breathing sensuality. At school her teachers considered her a brilliant pupil, following the lessons with ease, asking questions, passionate about literature. She loves thinking and talking. She is fourteen.

---

This talented young woman hones her intelligence on unexpected things for such a young pupil. She speaks of God and the requirements and rules he imposes on his followers. And her classmates listen to her, surround her with interest. She strolls the corridors of the school with the *Tawhid*, an Islamic philosophical work on the unity of God, in her hand.

In the morning when she passes through the school door, she takes off her veil and every day there is great fun with hair-does – corn-rows, afros, curls. Sometimes she hides in the toilets, then comes out again enveloped in her black outfit. Then she walks the corridors again, a shadow among the shadows, until a teacher on duty, or the head counsellor, reminds her about the prohibition and demands she remove her veil. So then, once again, she is sent to the principal's office where there are long discussions and debates about faith and liberty. And once again the authorities bring the law down on her while offering to compassionately listen and understand – but they are careful not to allow any intellectual value to her concepts.

Why does wearing the veil fascinate this young girl? If one puts to one side the easy answers to do with her naivety, her desire to oppose, her tendencies to be provocative, or whatever psychological characteristics, then one should look at the thoughts crystallised in this garment. Then one realises that these questions go beyond and englobe the girl, and that they also concern her teachers and all and sundry.

Before describing this scarf that hides the hair and the neck while leaving open the oval of the face, one should first note that the word *hijab* is an abstract term that in Arabic signifies an immaterial separation, like that between the profane and the sacred. So, during prayer, a *hijab*, traditionally translated as 'invisible curtain', separates the believer from 'those who do not believe in the future life' (Koran 17: 45). The correct translation of *hijab* should not be, in my opinion, 'curtain' or 'veil', but rather 'membrane'.

Besides, the same word, *hijab*, is used for the diaphragm, the partition between abdomen and thorax that has stirred the imagination since ancient times since it is the boundary between breath and viscera. In this sense, *hijab* should be seen as the equivalent of the Greek *phrenos*, meaning 'diaphragm' of course, but also the seat of the soul.[1]

In Arabic *hijab* also means 'amulet', the leather pouch in which the doctor or healer has inserted a fragment of the holy book. This talisman, which is supposed to be carried around the neck, arm or waist, envelops its users with a protective and invisible membrane that defends them from ill-will.[2]

So, *hijab* means an invisible membrane. By logical extension, the word also designates the 'hymen', that intimate membrane that is fundamental to Muslim marriage rites, but whose existence was unknown to the learned authorities for a long time. How can one demand a membrane be permanent if one doesn't know it exists? On the one hand, midwives always knew what the doctors didn't. On the other hand, in older times it was not a matter of a physical membrane, rather one of the separation conferred by the status of being a wife.

Just as many ideas can be found in the Greek word *hymen*, which in antiquity did not designate the biologists' real membrane, but actual marriage. '*Hymen, Hymenay!*' the crowd called out as the newlyweds passed. Married women had to cover their hair in public spaces. It was also the case that goddesses, 'virgins', or rather the unmarried (*parthenoï*) were represented bare-headed, like Athena or Aphrodite, while a veil covered the hair of the married Hera and Demeter. Thus it is that the Arab word *hijab*, 'subtle membrane', comes close to the original usage of the Greek word *hymen*, meaning both 'invisible membrane' and marriage.

A great number of Middle-Eastern cultures had, in any case, instituted the idea that married women should cover their hair. From the second millennium before Jesus Christ, Assyrians had a written law obliging married women to wear the veil, an idea taken up by the Greeks, who handed it on to the Christians and Muslims, and the last trace of it today is our 'bridal veil'.[3] This extends to our vocabulary, where we find the adjective 'nuptial', coming from the Latin *nubere*, meaning both 'to marry' and 'to be veiled'.

So, looking back over the history of costume and vocabulary, we find no ambiguity: being veiled means being married. What, then, is going on with these young women, veiled but single, who are increasing in numbers in our towns and suburbs? Just as with married women, their veil does not hide, it shows! It is another sign that they have an invisible membrane in them separating them from the ordinary.

Without being married, this young veiled girl professes and exhibits a philosophy; she proclaims that she belongs to a group whom she intends exclusively to endow with all her vitality, all her thoughts, all her love. Here the veil is not the mark of a repression of sexual life, but the announcement of a preliminary selection of candidates. Through her clothing this young girl announces that she is not available to anyone, only to some, those who share the same existential choices as her. And furthermore, far from putting off these selected candidates, she attracts them, precisely through the veil that has become a necessary condition of her seduction. We know that many of these young girls speak of the veil in terms of freedom or conquest, their right to choose the group of young men whom they authorise to court them.

The reading of the *hijab* needs to be revised, having for a while been led astray into a nostalgic thinking that interprets it as a will to hide one's charms because of submission to an archaic moral order. It should rather be understood, at least in European societies, as *a fashion* – that is, a way of presenting oneself that *distinguishes one from the common by being attached to a select group*. Distinction and belonging, that seems to be what the young woman who started our enquiry seems to be claiming.

The message has, moreover, been perfectly well understood and it unleashes anger and debates in a society where, in principle, no one is sexually inaccessible.

# 3
# *Filiation and Affiliation*

Raising his head, in that funereal heaven
He saw an eye, a great eye, in the night
Open, and staring at him in the gloom . . .
    Victor Hugo, *The Legend of the Centuries* [1877]

If there are no 'profiles' of 'personalities predisposed' to a 'radicalised' fate, as might be said, for example, of addictive or cyclothymic personalities, I have nonetheless noted a 'vulnerability to Jihadism' among young people whose personal and family history are both characterised by a deficit: *a weakened cultural identity in the first generation and an uncertain filiation in the second.*

One of many stories: The mother is a Spaniard from Castile. Her parents having separated when she was eight, she was put in the care of a grandmother who literally enslaved her. Schooled in an institution run by sadistic nuns, she went from the vindictive moods of the old woman to the institutionalised abuse of the Sisters. So, from her adolescence she ends up being equally disgusted by family and God. At the age of seventeen she heads off to France without papers, and gets a job in a household where she encounters a little warmth and understanding for the first time. Then she meets a man, a Spaniard like her from the same region. She likes the idea of an amorous relationship, but certainly not the rules and conventions. No question of getting married, giving in to the will of man, a third party – never again! The man is lazy and unfaithful to boot. They have a row, break up, get back together, break up again. After a final meeting she falls pregnant.

She curses and sticks up for herself. No one could say she holds her tongue! She still has the accent of her native land; they call it 'rocks and drums.' But the instinctive hatred she has towards her family has kept her at a distance from its cultural affiliations. She is clearly Spanish; she has the accent, but what else? She has a Catholic background and still remembers a few religious sayings. She might be a believer, but she never practises. She is always critical, with a caustic tongue and manner, always on edge, drawing attention through her vivaciousness and her acid opinions on the wickedness of the Church and the degradation of the world.

Coming out of her relationship with the man, the Spaniard of her first months in France, was a daughter whom she brought up alone. The daughter takes after her; beautiful and rebellious, also strong, sometimes violent, but so naive . . . and so flighty! The girl's father didn't acknowledge her, arguing that he was often away, so the child could have been anyone's. But the mother knows he is the one, suggesting a DNA test, which he refuses to take.

One day the mother finds a prayer mat in the nineteen-year-old's bedroom, along with Islamic clothing, a burqa, sarouel pants, and pamphlets that send her into a rage: 'How to be a Good Muslim', for example, or 'The Right Way to Read the Koran.' Her blood began to boil; she who had escaped the clutches of the viragoes in the convent, how could she lose her child to these sick veil-wearers? She demands an explanation. Her daughter stands up to her. She had converted six months ago. She pays visits to Muslims in prison. Later she learns that these young men her daughter has been visiting bearing sweets, clothing and mobile phones are suspected of belonging to jihadist networks.

It seems to me a typical story. Because of the mother's particular pathway through life, she saw herself as separated from her source – her source, not her 'roots'! The word 'roots' implies the existence of a static, and supposedly objective, reality. Roots, as in a tree. But humans are a long way from having that perfect way that trees flow from a carnal relationship with the earth. Nor do they have the instinctive intelligence of birds that, having flown thousands of kilometres, know how to find their way back to their natal nesting place on a branch or in a rocky crevice. No, humans have constantly to renew their origins, because for them *origins are not instinctive, but a combination of knowledge and will.* So, if one doesn't know one's origin, or play a part in it, cultivate it, then it will wither away or dry up like a spring. This is what happened to the mother who knew nothing about her Spanish origin and took no interest in it, through any customs or festivals. It is not just the past that makes origins, but also the present and the future. It is the spring one drinks at every day, being both of the place and from the place.

*Let us define this ever-flowing spring as something that takes an active part in the customs of a people, and that is itself active in its relations with other peoples.*

And here again, work on vocabulary will enrich our enquiry. In Arabic and in Hebrew, *'ain* means 'eye', in the basic sense of the organ of sight, but equally 'spring', no doubt because a pond shining brightly in the full sun can be thought of as the 'eye of the Earth'. And the word *'ain* designates the 'evil eye' as well, the eye suspected of being too bright, as it sends out poisonous rays of envy. So, from here we can understand the double meaning of the word *'ain:* the source that supports life, and the eye that keeps watch, envious and possibly poisonous.[1]

So 'source' is certainly the right word for both the flow that is indispensable for life, the source of life, and for magical surveillance and potential poison. To be cut off from one's source doesn't ever mean being cut loose, but rather being condemned, like Cain, to infinite wandering in the need to find another source, but always under the scrutiny of the owners of those places. Such is the case of the Spanish mother I have been discussing. She is always on the lookout for a new sense of belonging, but feels as if she has been handed over, defenceless, to the gaze of the envious.

Her daughter, having gone unacknowledged by her father, then instinctively refusing his belated attempts to get her back once she became an adult, has even less chance of attaching herself to her mother's source.

This girl is what I call a 'wandering soul'. She is not detached, since she has never been bound; not lost, since there is no place she has to find, no Ithaca to return to; but floating, anxious, filled with absence. She is a person ready to be taken, or taken over – she is prey to the hunters of souls.

---

*This, then, is one of the main characteristics that is a key to understanding the 'wandering souls' that have become easy prey to a growing religious radicality. This characteristic is declined across two generations: in the first, a functional break with the link to cultural belonging (the source), and in the second, problems of filiation.*

I was surprised by the frequency with which I encountered this characteristic in the long list – far too long – both of the young people who had carried out attacks in France, as well as in day-to-day clinical encounters.

But if this phenomenon is so obvious, others would have been able to see it before me. Or even instrumentalise it. The brains behind the jihad, those psychologists of partisan influence, have focused on the vulnerability of these people. They organise actual traps for souls, deftly combining philosophical and religious apprenticeships with more profane methods, alternating romantic seduction with promises of terrestrial paradise.

One of these thinkers is well known because his career and strategies have been subject to detailed analysis. Abu Mus'ab al-Suri[2] is the author of the voluminous 'Call to Global Islamic Resistance'. In this work he promotes a strategy of destabilisation in Europe, calling it the 'soft stomach of the West'. This work will be done by immigrant Muslim youth who are in a state of permanent revolt because they are not properly integrated.[3] So the priority is to conquer these young people.

We know that ideological action has become a priority among jihadic organisations. And while a thinker like al-Suri remains a point of reference in these milieus, many others have subsequently continued the work. They act, and also react, adapting their new forms of action to the protective measures taken by countries that have been targeted. That is how they noticed that populations that are receptive to the appeal of radicalisation were not exclusively composed of young Muslims, but could be joined by a not insignificant number of children who are unrelated to Islam, such as, in France, people from the Antilles, Africans of Christian background (coming out of the Cameroons, the Congo, Togo, the Ivory Coast, etc.); Mediterraneans from the South (Portugal, Spain, Italy),[4] Jews, especially Sephardic, whose parents had arrived in the 1960s, but also, quite often, people of 'mixed race' ['*métis*']. By 'mixed race' I mean the children of – sometimes unexpected – intercultural couples: Afghan and Antillese, Congolese and Italian, Algerian and Vietnamese, and many others. These children of modest origins, born in less integrated families, at a remove from integration by the accidents of life, unwanted, sometimes unwelcome. Each finds a personal invitation in this Islamic proselytising, a word that is directly addressed to them, like a promise to make amends. I feel their hearts beat faster, their heads spin. I hear them thinking: '*Finally! Here at last are people who take an interest in my existence.*'

In this way the Islamic call is sent out far and wide, on the waves of the internet, as well as through peer groups, siblings, among childhood friends, relayed by proselytising and activist cells that are spontaneously built up in the form of local organisations. There is surveillance, checks that every prayer has been properly done, every prohibition respected; relationships are checked, thoughts questioned, desires censored. This call circulates in a particular atmosphere, with attitudes, characterisations, expressions, a philosophy of everyday life, a sort of 'fashion'. Of course, the special targets, as Abu Mus'ab al-Suri had envisioned, are young Muslims, the children or grandchildren of immigrants from Algeria, Morocco or Tunisia. It is easier for them to be hooked since they imagine they are reconnecting with badly transmitted origins. This is how they become more Muslim than their parents, capable of teaching them things and correcting them. They themselves speak of 're-conversion', as in a *return*. Sometimes they are called 'born again', as we have come to call those newly converted into evangelical faiths.[5] In fact, this kind of 'return' can be found in most religions. In Hebrew the word for such returns is *teshuva*, which more precisely means 'response'. Maybe this is a case of a badly understood concept? Perhaps they think they already have answers to all their questions? But *teshuva* rather means 'God's response', not the one humans think they have found. Are they sure that God has replied to them?

And yet the Islamic call also reaches those young people, as I said, whose birth family (Christian, Jewish or agnostic) has nothing to do with Islam. It touches these young people, most often children of migrants as well, and even, though more rarely, the children of those we call 'ancestral French' [*Français de souche*]. So many 'wandering souls'. When they hear the call, varieties of *initiatory encounters*, or *ontological eurekas*, are set in motion.

The philosopher Philippe-Joseph Salazar notes that such a movement should be called by its name: it is a revolutionary dynamic, inasmuch as a revolution is a social movement capable of introducing a proselytiser into every household.

We can illustrate this with a quotation from the Gospels: 'And every one that hath forsaken houses, or brethren, or sisters, or father, or mother, or wife, or children, or lands, for my name's sake, shall receive an hundredfold, and shall inherit everlasting life' (Matthew 19: 29). As the prototype of revolutionary thought, militant Christianity addressed itself to one and all, transforming them into domestic revolutionaries. There is no revolution without this ideological burgeoning that brings a proselytiser to every hearth.

# 4
# *Conversion and Initiation*

And immediately something like scales fell from his eyes,
and he regained his sight. Then he rose and was baptized;
and taking food, he was strengthened.

Acts of the Apostles 9: 18–19

So, we are dealing with vacillating cultural identities
that end up encountering forces, powers or deities that
can make off with people and put them at their service. I
want to ask myself, despite the strange characterisation,
'who do these children belong to', these children or
grandchildren of migrants? Not to their ancestors, about
whom they have only a distant idea, almost as distant as
the literary, philosophical or political ancestors being
offered to them in school. Not to their parents, who
have often been excluded from filiation. These 'wandering souls' have sometimes completed long journeys
through the children's law courts and social services,
special assistance, refuges or foster families . . . so many
places, when they think about it, that make it that much
clearer to them how provisional their attachments are,

how precarious their modes of belonging. *Their identities are put on hold so many times.*

And now these 'wandering souls' discover at some
point, as they explore the internet or meet people in
the neighbourhood, that there are forces that recognise
them, point to them, rename them – above all rename
them! – and then offer *conversion* and *initiation*.

The family is Czech, Catholic, and it has been twenty
years since they migrated to France. The mother works
in a service company and the stepfather is a removalist.

Everything blew up when overnight the young man
in the family converted to Islam and quickly became
radicalised. He does his five prayers, obsessively reads
dozens of Islamic texts that he learns off by heart,
demands halal food, checks the meals his mother pre-
pares and spends his nights watching videos that show
the agony of Arabic children being bombed by the West.
He has also become very angry, seeks conflict, goes
destructively berserk on questions of politics. What's
more, he intends to convert his parents to the true law.
During an altercation with his mother, for example, he
called out: 'Islam is God.' Shocked, and being a fervent
Catholic, she retorted: 'You're mad!' Then the young
man threw himself on the ground and, still prostrated,
started raving exhortations against his mother's evil
words, begging God to pardon this poor woman and
save her from the fires of hell. At this point his mother
decided that he must be possessed. His parents tried to
reason with him, reminding him of what the Islamic
State was doing in Syria, but he screamed that this was
all propaganda, that it was the United States and France,
in conspiracy with the Jews and the Israeli State that

were spreading lies in order to grab the Arabs' lands and wealth. As far as he is concerned, Christianity is a false religion, mere idolatry, the proof being that satanic trinity . . . No! God is Islam! And once he realised he couldn't convert his parents, he gave in to rage and a kind of mystical despair at the idea that their souls are destined to *Shaitan* (Satan).

Abandoned by his biological father as a child, then accompanying his mother who had to run the gauntlet of immigration, a mother with distant attachments and periodic recourse to elements of traditional Catholicism, which no doubt made her who she was, this young man certainly fitted the definition I gave of the 'wandering soul', without attachments. His family had lost the functional link to its source, and he had lost the link to his own filiation.

But a 'wandering soul' doesn't wander for long. Is it even possible to conceive of someone without links? Of course not! Such people are necessarily always looking, lying in wait for the one who will appear one day as a bearer of a real force, the one who will come along to declare: '*I am interested in your existence!*'

In the past, before Islam, he tried to resolve his filiation problem via a first *initiation*. At the age of thirteen, he had joined a group that was keen on urban acrobatics (scaling buildings, daring jumps). This initiative, which at the time had gained him a certain local 'success' with his neighbourhood friends, ended in a failure. Before long he was no longer able to carry out his street acrobatics or building climbs. At the age of fourteen he began a serious cannabis habit, which not only diminished his physical capacities, but also had disastrous psychological effects, probably the origin of delusional episodes.

He had five years of intense hashish use, then he started having terrifying visual and auditory hallucinations. After that, psychiatric advice, and he agreed to treatment on antipsychotics. Then things seemed to settle down. After six months he stopped going to his psychiatrist. He had just started secretly to convert to Islam.

So, *conversion* came to take the place of psychiatric care, which had implicitly condemned the young man to an ordinary existence, taking him from the status of a child gifted with unusual capabilities (climbing the façades of buildings) to being deficient and, before long, on welfare. Not long afterwards, probably motivated by the desire to detoxify from cannabis, he passionately embraced radical Islam, in the first instance fascinated by on-line videos, then a group of his neighbourhood friends added texts, brochures and practical know-how.

The path this young man took seems to me characteristic of this surprising mixture of uncoupling (the 'wandering soul') and of revolt against *the banality of right-mindedness*. He might well be a 'wandering soul', but definitely not a psychiatric patient! He feels this very deeply. His pathway indicates that it would be hasty to give into ready-made conclusions by blaming only his lack of belonging; it correlates most often with an appetite for a surplus of thinking. These young people want their floating engagement in the world to introduce them to new worlds. And they intuitively perceive that genuine thought is necessarily adversarial. In other words, *thinking starts by thinking against* (against common thought, against the self-evident); those who think in a conformist way (as in the masses), are not thinking at all. Here, more than ever, *vox populi* is not *vox dei.* In short, these youngsters have the feeling that the problems they were born with should turn out to be the first moments of their future initiation.

During the coming of age initiations of 'traditional' societies, as classically described by ethnologists, the young are of course initiated, but into something they already are. This could be expressed in a kind of Nietzschean way as: '*One can only be initiated to oneself!*'[1]

For example, a young Beti from the Cameroons becomes Beti after having gone through the initiation rites (perhaps one should say: 'finally became Beti', the Beti that he already was). Because, having been born Beti, with a Beti mother and father, speaking the Beti language and beginning to delve into the subtleties of his culture and traditions, he wasn't actually Beti while he still hadn't been 'initiated'.[2] *We have to conclude from this that initiation cannot be reduced to learning something new, but reveals the very nature of the initiand.*

We can guess that the 'traditional' initiations found in Africa, America, Australia or New Guinea used to allow for (or still do among certain more or less isolated populations),[3] a robust affiliation of people, building up their cultural personality and their personal identity in the same movement. The processes through which this foundational event comes about are complex and surprising; they are certainly a mystery to the outside observer, especially to a modern.[4] For the initiand there is always *a great fear*; intellectual and often physical *violence*; marks on the body and sometimes sexual violence as well.[5] And yet these procedures, that might seem absurd, useless or even immoral to the outsider, are always working towards the same, perfectly explicit, goal: *to transform a nature, a 'being in the world', with no link to any explanation.* And in this these rites are 'radical pedagogies', even if today they may sometimes be thought of as acts of torture.

This way of transforming someone's 'nature' or identity by way of ritualistic intervention, and not teaching, makes any personal interpretation on the part of the initiand impossible. In fact, it would be absurd to transform a nature by way of explanation, opening it to the risks of debate, and possibly the rapid corruption of its content starting with the second generation. Consequently, initiation rites are far removed from any symbolisation. They don't carry any signification. This is why, incidentally, anthropological interpretations failed for a long time to come to terms with them.

So, initiation at puberty in a traditional setting has the function of transforming an 'ethnic nature' – being Beti, as in the above example. In that instance one becomes Beti by way of a rite that is often violent, seems absurd, resists any explanation and cannot be captured by any symbolic interpretation.

This phenomenon – as strange as it was once widespread – is summed up by the ubiquitous rule about *initiation secrecy*: '*What your eyes have seen, what your body has felt here, your lips may never divulge . . .*'

This has been glossed over with the often repeated claim that the secret is that there is no secret, which may well be true in the sense that there may be no esoteric revelation or some kind of passing on of a story, excepting, of course, the lived experience. The unsayable experience of having been through a strange rite that permanently attaches the person to a 'nature' and *produces a memory through its own power.* This experience, one that is so difficult to reconstitute, is the true 'secret' of initiation.

In the very logic of these 'traditional' initiations we rediscover the same anchoring points in the trajectories of radicalising youth. Asked about where they belong, they reply by referring to violence, to their joining a group of peers and to the secrecy requirement. Should we be thinking about traditional initiations as the model for the conversion of our young people to fundamentalist Islam? I doubt it, mainly because religion presents itself mostly as an intellectual system that solicits understanding and cohesion.

We know that in the case of Christianity one is not born into it but one becomes Christian through baptism. The child of a Christian mother and father is not Christian until he or she is baptised. Now, baptism – three-fold immersion in water – is a rite that is supposed to symbolise death and resurrection. The child's first nature (marked by original sin) dies in order to be reborn purified, in the same way as Christ's resurrection. Baptism can be reduced to a few symbolic gestures, as in the current Catholic one, where the priest is happy to sprinkle a few drops of holy water on the forehead of the child, or even, in evangelical rites, involving complete immersion of a willing adult in front of the whole congregation. In both cases the basic idea is the same: removing the original nature of the person to be converted via a purification rite, and allowing a new being to emerge – in this case a Christian.

We understand then, that religious conversion is the opposite of 'traditional' initiation since it is based on a manner of choice. One is conscious of choosing a kind of baptism as a way of joining a community. And if this baptism is administered shortly after birth, when children are not capable of understanding what is happening to them, as in the Catholic rite, it will only become effective with 'confirmation', when the subject, usually an adolescent, knowingly asks to join the community of believers. Religious conversion ultimately remains a *desired metamorphosis, a radical transformation of an inherited corrupt nature.* As some say: a *metanoia.*[6]

However, there is one point of overlap between initiation and conversion as affiliation mechanisms. Both take on the task of 'fashioning' the identity of the person – and this at a time when it isn't yet fixed, and what's more, disrupted by the biological turbulences of puberty. Initiations and conversions have often been used to treat certain disorders that we moderns consider to be of a psychological, if not psychiatric, nature. When, in a traditional world, someone becomes aware of a young person's erratic behaviour, it is not unusual for the elders to say, 'it's time he was initiated', allowing for the thought that 'if he becomes who he is', he will give up this childish behaviour. In worlds where initiation is the primary reference, the disorder is often interpreted as a lack of initiation.[7]

As for the relationship between conversions to Christianity and the healing of the sick, a simple scan of the Gospels and the Acts of the Apostles will convince the reader that this is the case. According to these texts, Jesus was above all a kind of healer, giving sight to the blind, making cripples walk and exorcising the wayward of their demons.[8] If the sick person, as Christ often says, is healed through their faith, then their healing will inspire faith in many others . . . in the surroundings, the

village, the neighbourhood, sometimes the whole city.[9]
Healing has always produced believers.

Hence the saying, true despite its paradoxical inflec-
tion: '*You aren't cured because you believe; you believe
because you were cured – or because someone else has
been cured!*'

Now it becomes clear that the young Czech succes-
sively turned to both procedures, *initiation* first when
he was scaling buildings, and then later *conversion* to
Salafist Islam, in an apparent attempt at self-therapy.

Looking back at the trajectories of the young radicalised
people that I have had the occasion to meet, I am unable
to say if they were cases of initiation or conversion.
I rather see a hybrid of the two, an unexpected and
double-acting modern hybrid: an *initiatory conversion,*
so to speak. Because while they are certainly cases of
religious conversion, they do not satisfactorily answer
intellectual or moral questions. The person joins the
movement, then has a revelation on their 'true' nature.
That is why these 'initiatory conversions' depend on
strange new sensations, discoveries, sudden understand-
ings, genuine insights. If it happens that radical Islamic
conversions begin with curiosity, a period of finding
things out, sometimes through Web searches or read-
ings, they are made more concrete through friends,
'brothers', imams or activist proselytisers putting things
into perspective. They are activated through practical
advice from a charismatic personality, a guide, a leader,
someone who is always to be found in the young person's environment. This is the case for many of these
conversions, even – and perhaps above all – in the cases
of young people who have been raised in families with a

Muslim tradition. When it comes to radicality, there are only converts.[10]

*Being introduced to Islamic radicality is not just a simple religious conversion*, that is, the choice of a new faith, *but the simultaneous discovery of truths,* in the first place about oneself, and then about the world. *It is a matter of both conversion and initiation.*

Take this young girl: Her parents are Italian Catholics. On the death of her much-loved grandmother, she feels the need to pray. Her parents' Christianity seems to her to have lost any vitality. She can't remember a single prayer from the few months of catechism that she went through at the age of ten. She talks of this with a neighbourhood friend she likes to chat with or swap secrets. Her friend, who is Muslim, the child of Algerian immigrants, suggests prayers in Arabic, but first she would have to convert. Convert . . .? Perfectly simple, her friend assures her. All you need is two witnesses while you recite the articles of faith, repeating ritual phrases, and that's it! Why does she do it? No doubt there is the play element, but also the desire to experience the world. And so here we have a young girl, who used to be wracked by sobs when she thought of her grandmother, now feeling quite serene. Her friend offers to guide her through some explanations. Prayers, five times a day, ritual acts, ablutions, food restrictions. Later she introduces her to some young people of the faith who know the Koran by heart. And this young girl who was asking herself, 'How is it that Muslim prayer alleviates my sadness?' can provide the answer herself: 'Because it is true!'

One cannot underestimate the power of the revelation that accompanies this type of conversion, as if a veil were torn from the eyes, the sensation that now all is explained, oneself and the world. In the case of this young girl, questions that were quite simple on the surface concealed the impenetrable enigma of her own origins. A far-away Italy that her parents never visited, never wanted to talk about, with every chance of a large family of uncles, aunts and cousins whom she doesn't know. A complex and rich world to which her deceased grandmother would occasionally allude. And now she is gone, leaving her alone . . . Then comes the conversion, which, in a quick turnaround, places the enigma in the future rather than in the past.

Another story: This one is about a young man of about twenty who lives alone with his mother. She is intelligent, speaks at least six languages, knows her culture, her neighbours' cultures, and that of her adopted country perfectly well. She is an ethnic Senufo from the Ivory Coast. When she met her son's father, who was also Senufo, but from Burkina, they were madly in love, planning to get married, making plans for the future. She fell pregnant. But her lover's father opposed the relationship, and overnight the man disappeared. She migrated to France, found work, brought up her child alone. But this handsome little boy who was so quick, so intelligent at primary school, suddenly changed once he got to high school. He began to smoke hash at twelve, then dealing, theft, snatching mobile phones. And all of a sudden at seventeen, coming out of yet another hearing before the juvenile court, he confesses to his mother that he has converted to Islam and asks her to join him in his faith. She vehemently refused. After that she tries to find a way of getting him back to her country, where he has never been, to put him through traditional Senufo initiation, which she had never spoken to him about.

For the young man's part, he speaks of his conversion as an illumination of his being. Now he understands why his father left him before he was even born, why he has stumbled from one catastrophe to another, why he can't manage to kick his cannabis habit, or his addiction to video games, why, most of all, he feels foreign, different from other kids, different from his mother as well, from the beginning. All these trials, he thinks, were his preparation for future illumination: his meeting with Islam. A eureka feeling, a total upheaval, pregnant with possibilities.

All at once the convert has an intuition about his destiny, and an immediate knowledge about the real way the world is organised.

Adults who meet young radicalised people are sometimes revolted, and sometimes fascinated by this unexpected attachment, this violent metamorphosis of their being. They try to argue with them, contradict them or reason with them, all to no avail, *because their conversion is not a problem, not a symptom, it is a solution!* It is even a double solution, one bearing on their personal problems, and one for their disconnected family that they mean to integrate with the way the world is going, saving it from wandering.

Certain things may have been present in the life of the young person ever since childhood (problems of identity, uncertainty about who one is, questioning of one's 'properties') and remain somewhat in the background for years, only manifesting perhaps in distress or anti-social behaviour. They can also result in illness. So, conversion can draw in even more force to the extent that it substitutes for psychological confusion, even hallucinatory or full-blown psychotic episodes.

In the local elementary public school that I went to in rue Pasteur, Gennevilliers, half the students, probably more, in my fourth year class must have been immigrants. That was 1959–1960, nearly sixty years ago now. I don't know what became of them, what paths they took to join our society moving, as always, along crooked lines. I learnt, incidentally, that several died prematurely, victims of overdoses or AIDS, and two were killed during an attempted prison break. Anyone who has read Victor Hugo knows that when the poor try to revolt they have every chance of an unhappy ending.

We lived in 'estates', that only later would become *quartiers*. We turned the town into a village, playing in the streets, shooting for goal between cars blowing their horns. We took over cellars and rooftops, transforming them into caves for sexual initiation. This was an effervescent, youthful, zest for life, straddling any anxieties about the end of the world; because the world we had been born into was already gone, and its absence could be read in our breathless excitement. Our childhood remained one of astonishment; our adolescence was on fire, fuelled by its tense relation with the last moments of the sexual morality of an earlier era. Our twenties were political. We were passionate Marxists, up in arms against the injustice of American imperialist aggression causing such suffering in Vietnam. I was a member of the 'grassroots Vietnam committee', opposed to the 'national Vietnam committee' ... huge clashes over little differences! Just like the young Czech man I spoke of earlier, we signed up after seeing photographs of martyred children. For us too, the centre of the world was over there, not in Raqqa, Bamiyan, Teheran, Gaza or Mecca, but in Cuba, Hanoi or Peking. We couldn't see our own front steps because of our gaze fixed on the distance. We gave up our local affiliations in order to join a world of equals, crafted on a planetary scale. The only difference, in my opinion, between their twenties and mine is that the people we decided to join forces with had no interest in us. We were even a bit of a nuisance to them. No recruiters, no networks – no internet of course! – no regiments of foreign soldiers, no invitations for pioneering dreamers. We didn't know what road to take to join the world revolution. Yet this was the word on every lip, the one we went to sleep with and woke in the morning saying, '*join the revolution*', but where? Vietnam? Impossible! South America, then? Some went, as we know, but under their own steam.

At the time I had no idea I had the same problems as the radicalised youth I am describing, the social symptoms of disaffiliation. My family was deeply disturbed by its one-way migration, but its sense of belonging remained strong and calm, without conflict. Nevertheless, it wore away day by day, through distance and isolation. At the time, I had little interest in the elders. I was much more interested in my comrades, in a world on the move, in building a universal community. We fail to notice that children are much more interested in other children than in their parents. I wouldn't say that my Marxist allegiance was anything like a *conversion*, but there is no doubt it distanced me from the traditional duties towards my ancestors, and it blocked the path towards faith, worship and rituals. I was a 'wandering soul', and probably have remained one to the extent I am still vulnerable to ideologies.

I know that cultural belonging, what my teacher, the originator of ethnopsychiatry Georges Devereux, called 'ethnic identity', *is not natural; it is willed.*[11] I learned that affiliation, the fact of being 'initiated' into a prescribed universe, is a blessing when one is guided by elders. Modern countries, these huge spaces that bring heterogeneous populations together under the same law, are duty bound to provide answers to questions that a self-declared laicity thinks it has resolved, haunting questions that I notice among the radicalised young, the same questions that were once mine. I set them out here in logical order:

– Are we just human beings? What I mean is, are we just made from the coupling of two human beings that are our mothers and fathers, as common-sense ideology lets it be understood? Are there not other ingredients going into identity? We know this from the facts: places (country, village, neighbourhood), languages (from the generation we are born into, as well as those of preceding generations),[12] divinities (the greater ones that are instituted in churches, plus the no less important local deities, saints, the dead, shrines and springs) and all the numerous, complex rituals. No! No society can be satisfied with humans who are just simple biological beings.

– And furthermore: are we simply constituted by our origins? Isn't identity more like a work in progress? Isn't it possible to choose one's identity, just as today one can choose one's sex? Isn't it possible to change it, constitute a new identity for oneself? And, as the case may be, through conversion . . . to what Church? In submitting . . . to what kind of initiation? And if it is possible to choose one's identity, how then does that articulate with the laws of the land?

– And the third question, whose ripples spread out to touch not only the family, but society, the country, this France that most of the converted know in a visceral sense since childhood, but with which they hold an ambivalent relationship, sharing a common substance, yet feeling cut from a different cloth: *if someone resolved to reveal hidden gods, local gods and ancestral gods, gods from here and gods from yonder; if he or she resolved to reactivate forgotten, prohibited, rites, would that necessarily mean being engulfed once again in that terrible war of the gods that we have been looking to avoid for centuries?*[13]

As we have now come to realise, the questions that the Islamic converts field are not simply of an affective or 'symbolic' order; they are genuine metaphysical questions. The radicalised youth are not just 'wandering souls' captured by perverted gurus, political opportunists or mad tyrants of the apocalypse. They are also seekers, desirous for meaning, hunting for answers to fundamentally philosophical questions.

# 5
# *Apocalypse*

Nous sommes la jeunesse ardente
Qui vient escalader le ciel.
Dans un cortège fraternel
Unissons nos mains frémissantes,
Sachons protéger notre pain.
Nous bâtirons un lendemain
Qui chante.[1]

Paul Vaillant-Couturier, *Jeunesse* (song), 1937

He was born in a Teke village, near Pointe-Noire in the Congo. His mother died bringing him into the world. They would say, in that part of the world, that he came 'against his mother', that he had killed her. How can such a heavy charge be brought against an infant a few days old? They knew who his father was, of course. He was generous, never failing to bring presents when he paid his mistress a visit. But after the woman died, no one ever saw him again. The boy had no brothers or sisters; his mother had lost all her previous babies. So the child was put in the care of an aunt, actually one of the mother's cousins. And so he grew up among his cousins, knowing he was different, and he was not allowed to forget it. When an adult had an accident, it was his fault, and when a woman died of an illness, it was him again. He was even put on trial when he was five. He was forced to confess that he was a sorcerer, that he 'ate people at night'.[2] He was good at school, however, well-behaved, no outbursts or mischief . . . So why would anyone have anything against him?

One day a grand-aunt, a distant relative of his grandmother's generation, came on a family visit to the village. She saw him wandering about, thin, looking lost, wild-eyed. She took pity on him. Then she decided to take him back to France, where she had emigrated. He was ten, maybe eleven. No one remembered the exact date of his birth. She enrolled him in her local school, in her suburb, and made a special effort of kindness to get him used to his new environment. But, truth be told, he never succeeded. She thought that maybe city life didn't suit him, or at least he was missing his village, even though he was a punching bag, a scape-goat. Ten years later, she herself had to bring it to his attention, he was frightening her so much. He had converted to an aggressive kind of Islam, and no longer wanted to speak to *koufars*, deniers of the true faith. He spent his evenings with his new friends, all dressed in traditional clothing, combing the streets targeting the impious God-haters. But what terrorised his grand-aunt to the point of prompting her to seek help was a scene that lasted an entire night. She had brought up, once again, the fact that there were no ties with Islam in their family, that they were Christians, Catholics, had been for generations. Yes, they were once animists, maybe some still were, but Muslim? Never! They started to scream at each other. He lifted his arms towards the heavens, then moved towards her in a menacing fashion. The end of the world is nigh. She would have to convert without delay, otherwise she would go and burn in hell for millennia.

You may be surprised to find anxieties among young modern people, coming straight out of antiquity. Such as the apocalypse. It is now their turn, following so many others in the past in times of radical change, to repeat that the end of the world is imminent.[3] Yet again, God will destroy nearly every living being. Only a few of the just, a few 'perfect ones' will survive, or alternatively, according to other versions, will be brought back from the dead. The rest will disappear in a gigantic purification and go to roast for eternity. They want to save their loved-ones – be it a mother, a sister or a brother – who run the risk of sinking with all the detritus of a condemned world, for the sole reason that they weren't aware of God's decision. They spread the word, give warning, militate, preach, scream with rage that no one is listening.

But how can they be so certain that the apocalypse is imminent? Because they have been instructed how to read the warning signs – signs that, as far as they are concerned, are totally unequivocal.

The first of these signs is corruption. Corruption in the world, breakdown in human relations, or among countries, a general corruption in the nature of living beings. The Koran even notes that at the end time the difference between humans and animals will disappear, at which point animals will speak, telling humans where

Overview

they went wrong. The social order will also be inverted, as far as we can work out from the prophet Jibreel's long hadith, where Mohammed thus describes the warning signs:

> *The slave girl will give birth to her mistress, and you will see the barefoot, the naked, the destitute, and the shepherds vying with each other in building.*

Above all, disintegration of the sexual order. Sex will become banal. Intercourse will no longer be for starting a family, but just for nothing, any time, any place, even in public in view of passers-by. 'Bizarre' forms of sexuality will be practised, homosexuality, bestiality, every kind of perverse coupling. The family will disappear. Boys will defy their fathers. Women will give birth to daughters who will treat them like servants. Adultery will be normal, divorce obligatory, to the point that children will not know who their fathers and mothers are.

These presaging signs, come to think of it, could all be related back to a foundational Surah, number 49, *Al-Hujurat*:

> O you mankind, surely We created you of a male and a female, and We have made you races and tribes that you may get mutually acquainted. Surely the most honourable among you in the Providence of Allah are the most pious; surely Allah is Ever-Knowing, Ever-Cognizant.

The meaning of the text is clear: differences pertaining to sex, social status, language and custom are the result of divine will. What we are invited to conclude from this is that creation is manifest in the ordering of differences. Any act that tries to modify or do away with them, and consequently any fabrication of a hybrid, will let loose the wrath of God, like the biblical story of the flood. And now humans are faced once again with the apocalypse, that is, the *destruction of the world* and the *revelation of the truth of creation*.

These are actually the two meanings of the word apocalypse, the most common being that of 'general catastrophe' and the 'end of the world', but there is also the learned meaning, conforming with its Greek etymology, of 'revelation'.

So we can guess that apocalypse is therefore another way of telling the story of the world's creation.

When time began, the Yoruba story goes, Olodumare the god of creation, as soon as he separated from the world with which he had been at one, grabbed hold of a strange object: *'a stone that, the further it was thrown, the closer it fell'*.[4] The handling of this stone gives birth to the world; a definition of 'time o', that inconceivable beginning that recedes the closer one gets to it.[5] Such is the origin of the Yoruba world, which has nothing at all to do with the work of an artisan, as in the monotheistic bibles. Their initiation is the same, a beginning endlessly begun again, a perpetual renewal of origins. They are initiated shortly after birth; on their name day; at puberty, of course; upon meeting their tutelary gods; at the birth of their first child; on the occasion of important deaths; at their own death; and after death during the stages of ancestralisation. Each time, each sequence of social life is a beginning, each scansion the occasion for a new birth. Until death, itself conceived of as a new birth, an initiation to the world of the dead. And for the most deserving of the dead, some may in the end be born afresh, to the rank of ancestor.

---

*Polytheistic* worlds, like that of the Yoruba, have totally embraced the logical link between the beginning and end of the world. That is, if the beginning is inconceivable, then the end must be just another beginning, the arrival of a universe where any human can become a god and where some deities come to join humans to the point of possessing them, and initiations are the occasion for this. In this way, certain dead people (ancestors protecting their family line, who are honoured by their descendants) can elevate themselves to the status of deity, in the family, the clan or the village.

In this way, social life carries on according to the creation myth; the beginning is at the end, and the end is always a new beginning. 'Cyclical time' is sometimes used to designate these worlds where myths are still vital. But the term is too imprecise. Time is not naturally cyclical; it is rendered cyclical by the process of initiation – an intense social activity designed to construct an indefinite 'eternal return'.

In monotheistic mythologies, time becomes linear, stretching out towards a goal that is the creation of the world by a demiurge who expects perfection. In this way monotheisms have produced the notion of progress, but also evidence of an end of times – *the world having been created by a first act, will now necessarily be destroyed by a final one.* This is predicted in all sorts of ways: religious, of course, social and revolutionary, military (nuclear anxiety), ecological (climatic anxiety). In certain respects, monotheism is a curse. Because, instead of ancestralisation, that exists here only for exceptional beings (the pantheon of remarkable personalities), what appears to be developing increasingly and more violently is an apocalyptic theory.

---

The French revolution was an apocalypse, a revelation about the truth of history, just like the Bolshevik revolution, and naturally, the Islamic revolution that is calling our radicalised young people. This apocalypse that has stunned them, which only a few of the chosen will survive, which precedes the advent of widespread Islam, is the monstrous child of a world devoid of ancestors.

Among the three monotheistic religions are quite a few apocalypses: Ezekiel's first of all, John's (the most famous), but also the Muslim apocalypses which come later. They are all characterised by the expectation of a Messiah, someone new and as yet unknown, as with the Jews, or the return of a former one, Jesus, Mahdi, the hidden imam. But in order to grasp the logic, I will spend a little time on the very first (or at least in the logic of the biblical story), the one who lies at the foundation of the others, certainly the most famous: the story of Noah.

So, once the Earth had been created, and the world now existed, and humans had named the plants and animals, *then* all sorts of problems began to emerge.

Noah, called *Noa'h* in Hebrew because the biblical text has it that *yenahamenu*, 'he shall console us' . . . We have to understand: 'After the announcement of the catastrophe, the Flood, *'he shall console us.'* He who endured the anger of God, will know how to bring relief to terror among his fellow men.

Upon the death of his father, Lemekh, at the age of seven hundred and seventy-seven years, Noah was five hundred years old. This was the time when men were multiplying in all directions over the Earth and were coupling in an anarchic fashion. '. . . the sons of God saw the daughters of men that they were fair; and they took them wives of all which they chose' (Genesis 6: 2).

Who are these strangers ravishing the daughters of men? 'The sons of *Elohim*', it is written. It is thought they are a kind of demi-god, perhaps secondary gods since they are called *Elohim*, which in Hebrew means 'deities' or 'lords'. Certainly superior beings, without moral scruples when it came to their sexual choices. They coupled without distinction, being eternally priapic, ithyphallic, taking as many virgins as married women, men and even animals. Certain passages of the text do not exclude the idea that vegetables and minerals were not spared their reproductive enthusiasm.

So God was moved to anger for the first time and, as punishment, reduced the life-span of humans to only a hundred and twenty years. But neither men nor other beings heard the warning.

Here the text is more precise on what is meant by the beings who are mixed up with men. They are called *Nephilim*, literally meaning 'fallen' in Hebrew (Rashi, the celebrated eleventh-century commentator claims that they are called *Nephilim* because they made men 'fall', or brought about the Fall). And these Nephilim were not content to just have sexual relations with women, beasts and things, they engendered children. God explodes in anger. He regrets having created the world, and 'his heart was deeply troubled'. So he decided to wipe from the face of the earth every living thing – 'both man, and beast, and the creeping thing, and the fowls of the air' (Genesis 6: 7). Because, as the text says, 'the wickedness of man was great in the earth'. Only Noah found favour in the eyes of God, and it is to him he announces the destruction to come, the apocalypse: *the deluge.*

What interests me here is neither the destruction, which we have seen is necessarily 'called for' by the idea of creation by a demiurge, nor the flood, nor even the saving of a core group of 'pure' couples who will bring about a renewed humanity, but the motives for God's anger, what it was that made him decide to destroy the world. If we are to believe the text, the soiling that revolts him is *hybridisation*, the mixing of species and categories. This is corrupting the order he created. This is why Noah will invite paired animals into the Arc. No more mixing! From now on it will be giraffe with giraffe, lion with lioness, billy-goat with nanny ... If you think about it, God's anger comes from the fact that the hybrids engendered by these couplings are a creation that exclude him. A creation invented by the creatures themselves.

Now, creation – and creativity as well perhaps – is the sole province of God. Humans in Noah's time sinned through *hubris*, a Greek word usually translated as 'excess' and which in this case links up with its close-homonym, *hybrid*. These creatures took over the principal function of creation by allowing themselves to hybridise men and deities, engendering new forms, monsters in the thousands.

Hence, based on the analysis of the first apocalypse, that of Noah, we can see how the monotheistic world must end. Started with an act of the creator, it will finish with his own anger once the creatures have taken over his creative function. So we can ask what kinds of hybridisations our young radicals are anticipating, taken over as they are by the imminence of a new apocalypse.

Who among all the children who grew up in the Claude-Debussy Estate in Gennevilliers, that mini-ghetto of Jewish Egyptian refugees in France, too young to be aware of their exile, was able to accomplish the millenarian prescription that is inscribed in the Koran to respect other nations or other tribes? There is a simple answer: none! Egyptian Jew, son of Egyptian Jews, grandson, and so on, of Egyptian Jews from time immemorial, how could I in turn engender Egyptian Jews? And even if that did happen, where would my children find, in turn, Egyptian Jews to marry while the community has disappeared, been eradicated, its members expelled and exiled to the very last one? Even those, among the children of the Estate, who found within it a wife or a husband, were unable to turn their kids into Egyptian Jews. The world they were immersed in was now so different: first of all, the language, and the atmosphere, and the earth, and the way the wind blew. And whatever called them outside . . . Rather, most were carried away by the hotheadedness of youth and left their little community, and always through love. They linked up with other migrants, from Africa, Asia, the south of Europe, migrants from the provinces, from the Gers, Picardy or Bretagne. They had no choice but to beget hybrids, to the point of seeing themselves as such. So, it is no surprise that, in May '68, they read the unfolding apocalypse as a message addressed to them in person? I myself was on all the barricades.

Unthinkable short-circuit between today's violence and yesterday's mythologies! I am beginning to think that the obviousness of the apocalypse comes to these young people by way of being constantly subjected to an irrepressible call to mix.

# 6
# Hashish and Assassins

Religious suffering is, at one and the same time, the expression of real suffering and a protest against real suffering. Religion is the sigh of the oppressed creature, the heart of a heartless world, and the soul of soulless conditions. It is the opium of the people.[1]

Karl Marx, *A Contribution to the Critique of Hegel's Philosophy of Right*

When cows are sick, they will spontaneously swallow cannabis leaves and after a long sleep wake up cured. Humans might have taken up this substance after watching animals make use of it as a hypnotic and as a basic treatment for existential uneasiness. I have often been told a story, which I heard for the first time on the Island of Reunion, where they call the plant *zamal* – a word of Madagascan origin, deriving, they tell me, from the Arabic *jamal*, 'beauty'. Unless it is a creole word that might mean 'for treating animals in pain'. French, at least from the nineteenth century, incorporated the word *haschish* from the

Arabic word that means 'fodder [*fourrage*], hay for cattle'.[2]

Perhaps this name 'fodder' indicates through its insignificance that appearances can be deceptive, that what one thinks is 'grass' (another of its many names) is actually not hay at all, that this plant might have a hidden force, hidden behind a deliberately ordinary name. Because *hashish* is indeed a power, a plant endowed with a power that is hard to pin-point. You might examine its leaves, flowers or seeds in vain; the power remains imperceptible. You have to choose the right time to harvest, keep only the female plants, dry them, sieve them to separate the droplets of resin that are then packed into goat-skin bags to enrich it. Then the resin is heated, not too much to avoid sending it up in smoke, but enough to soften it for compressing. Later on, consumable products are derived: oils, butters, powders – with strong, nauseous odours. While cows might instinctively perceive the effects, us less sensitive humans have had to experiment for a long time, dedicating ourselves to complex preparations, before enjoying the properties of the plant. This factual description might give the impression that the power of cannabis is neutral, that it can be appropriated without problem. It has strength [*puissance*], of course, but without intentional power [*pouvoir*] . . . This positivist account of the plant strikes me as insufficient, to say the least.

Psychotropic plants can be classed in two categories, based on what different peoples do with them. There are those that are gods in themselves, and those that constitute vehicles towards hidden worlds, where there are sorcerers, spirits or gods. Coffee is a kind of god, even today. In Ethiopia sacrifices are made to it; just like tobacco in Native America, or wine among the ancient Greeks and Romans.[3] But coca, on the other hand, is above all a vehicle that allows the shepherd in the Andes to travel without fatigue in high altitudes, and the shaman to move around in the spirit world. As for the powerful hallucinogenic Datura, which certain south American Indians administer even to new-borns, it is said to 'open the eyes' so one can attend to the dangers of the night, that is, the hidden world which has hostile intentions.[4] Then there is the peyote cactus of the Huichol Indians that gives visions of the future.[5]

The power of plants has been considered, in our society since antiquity, as akin to that of the gods, and very often in traditional societies. And gods have intentions, as we know, even if they are not clear to humans. Drugs and gods ... still linked in the nineteenth century in Marx's well-known phrase, which denounced religion as the 'opium of the people',[6] a formulation whose opposite would be equally true. Because in many places, it has to be said, opium is the religion of the people. Georges Devereux, for his part, attached a third term to Marx's saying, *ideology*, as powerful as the gods and as toxic as a drug.[7]

He drove his parents so mad with worry with his non-stop hash smoking, that at first his conversion to Islam seemed like a good thing. These parents didn't have the slightest religious connection, just a vague humanist morality. They were 'ancestral' French. Their ancestors were no doubt Catholic three or four generations ago, then they became communists, and finally atheists in the generation before theirs, then nothing. In the throes of passion, they decided to live together at the age of

twenty. She came from a well-off bourgeois family; his
came from a more clerical milieu. The families were
opposed to their relationship. But faithful only to their
desire, they intended to tie the knot for life. They got
married. He knew that she was a little flighty. She didn't
care a bit that he was a little obsessive. They took a
while to have a child. He was thinking about his career;
she, still bohemian, was enjoying life. The child came
into their lives seven years after they were married. As
the baby grew in the womb, so did their anxiety. Had
they taken stock of this responsibility? She started to go
out more often; with her girlfriends, she claimed. He
scowled, closed in on himself, ruminated in solitude.
He tended to blame himself for his nonchalance; she
couldn't stand his lack of empathy. One evening when
she was out once again, he went through her stuff and
came upon her diary. He was completely flabbergasted
by what he read and sat there as if paralysed. She had
never stopped seeing the lover who had preceded him.
And that very night she had gone off to see him again.
He kept turning over his sombre thoughts for a long
time . . . betrayal, lies, secret meetings, absences. Then
he fixed on an idea. He couldn't let it go; it kept coming
back. The child she was carrying, the son he was hoping
for, maybe it was another man's . . .

That night he should have dropped everything and
left. For years he blamed himself for staying. But his son
was to be born the following month. How could he just
abandon him without even seeing him?

Is it for all these reasons that this unwelcome child
was never able to 'find his place'? That he had so many
difficulties from the very first moments of life? He was
small, puny, often crying, and sickly. He was late learn-

ing to walk, talking as well, and at every subsequent stage in life. He repeated a year in primary school and in early secondary as well. He hated school; it was always a martyrdom for him. He only lasted a year in upper secondary. The gap between him and the other students was so clear and so humiliating, that he developed a phobia about it. At this point he began to smoke hash. He began to smoke continually, and always a lot, maybe ten joints a day. He spent his nights smoking and playing on his computer. He became unstable, abusive, violent and sometimes incoherent. At this point he ran into the group, probably on-line, or simply in the street. And then he converted to Islam.

At this early stage, his parents thought it was good development. He had friends for the first time. He began to go out, even if it was mostly at night. He spoke to his parents as well, a lot, but it was always about God, Allah. He wanted to convince them he had made the right choice. They, who had been careful not to give him any religious guidance ('when he is grown up, he can make up his own mind!'), didn't know how to react. When he started on political questions, telling them in great detail about Dieudonné videos,[8] explaining to them the evil things the Jews and Americans were getting up to, they started to get worried. What could they do? Send him to a psychologist? He had seen plenty of them when he was a kid. He didn't want to hear about it. What, then? . . . Wait . . . Hope . . .

He was picked up in Turkey when he and two of his friends were in the process of trying to meet up with the Daesh troops.

'A wandering soul waiting for an owner', I said earlier, excluded from filiation (at least in his father's mind) in a family that has been broken down for several generations, even though it was 'native.' You might well ask what the place of the hash is in all of this!

Because of its relaxing and analgesic qualities, cannabis relieves psychological tensions. But, as the effects wear off, the substance leaves the users more anxious than before they took it, which leads to further intoxication, and so on. It is much harder to get over the pleasure than the suffering, the relief than the anxiety. When the user wants to get out of this vicious circle, but finds himself incapable of giving up the good feeling produced by it, he looks for some kind of support to help him give up. This is the point where the user may venture into mystical practices, the point where our young man met radical Islam.

We know that Islam prohibits the ingestion of any substance that might hinder concentration during prayer (alcohol, as well as drugs). I imagine the first request he had of his new faith was to rid him of his dependency.

A legend brought back by Marco Polo has been circulating in the West ever since the thirteenth century. Hassan Ibn al-Sabbah, 'the old man of the mountain' as he was called at the time, the last upholder of initiatory Islam, founded a Shiite sect in 1090, the *Nizaris* or the *Batinians* (from the Arabic *baten*, entrails, since the members of the sect advocated an esoteric, hidden, 'visceral' interpretation of the Koran).

According to this legend, the old man of the mountain, perched in his mountain fortress at Alamut, 2,100 metres high, initiated young men into both his doctrine and knowledge of the world. After he had them take vast quantities of hashish, he led them into a garden where they could partake, under their cannabis intoxication, of all the pleasures that life allows, of the table and of the flesh. After they were brought back unconscious to their cells, they were made to believe on awakening that they had just spent time in paradise. And if they wanted to go back, they had to carry out a mission that would be given them, without asking a single question. These were assuredly suicide missions, since they left Alamut like Sicarian raiding parties, driving into the heart of the enemy camp to assassinate princes or generals. Hence the name they were supposedly given, the *'hashashin*, 'consumers of hashish' in Arabic. This word went into Italian as *assassino*, giving the French and other derivations.

If we are to believe this legend, then Hassan Ibn al-Sabbah would be the inventor of modern terrorism, which opposes possessed individuals, indifferent to their own death, to regular armies. We saw them (re)emerge in the Iran–Iraq war of 1980–1988, then they multiplied during the Gulf and Middle-Eastern wars, and today in the combats between Daesh and its numerous foes. This creation of terrorism took place under the aegis of a substance: hashish. The reign of terror Hassan Ibn al-Sabbah imposed through 'targeted assassinations' carried out by a handful of faithful with death as their ally prevailed for decades over significant armies, for instance the Turkish Seljuks and the Crusades.[9]

Perhaps Baudelaire was also thinking of the old man of the mountain when he wrote, 'He would be angel; he became an animal.' At least that was the way he described one of the effects of hashish in *Les paradis artificiels*.[10]

By the way, can hashish – which consumes people to the point that they lose their will, which modifies their perception of time and the body, which changes their way of being in the world – recruit for a cause? This is an unlikely hypothesis, attributing as it does an intention to a plant, strategies to a substance.

Yet on a long-term basis, after several years of intense intoxication, this substance, because of the daily repetition in the same sequence, mechanically establishes a link between two opposed states: *euphoric bliss, coming from the removal of tension, and unbridled violence, to the point of self-sacrifice when the effects have worn off.* This was already the model of the legend that Marco Polo brought back.

I don't know how much historical truth there is in this legend, but it describes a plausible mechanism. And even if it were only a legend, its constant retelling has given rise to many political and mystical sects over the centuries, and perpetuated a model for terrorism right through to the present day.

# 7

# *Terror*

He who wears golden *culottes* is the enemy of the *sans-culottes*. There are only two sides, the corrupt and the virtuous.

> Maximilien Robespierre at the Jacobins' Club,
> 8 May 1793

Modern psychology thought it had gotten rid of the concept of *terror* thanks to the magic of a concept, that of 'trauma', a concept that has been duly broadened, covering a multitude of feelings and classifying them under this same medical, technical, flat word. From the outset, 'trauma' confuses three 'states' a shocked person can be in, which ordinary language is happy to distinguish as terror, fright and fear. In other words, when we think of a person undergoing trauma, are we speaking of the effect of their fear, fright or terror?

*Terror* is a powerful word that almost acts without its referent. It is enough to announce one's terror for it to be unleashed all around. In French it is impossible to avoid the political connotations since it has come to designate an historical period, as everyone remembers, during the bloodiest years of the French revolution (1793–1794). What is terror?

Terror is not a feeling. You can't sense it. You are invaded by it, thrown to the ground, appalled. Nor is it an emotion, but a more archaic phenomenon, a spreading paralysis that freezes body and soul. Its equivalent in the animal world might be playing dead – like those garden spiders that curl up as if dead when cornered by a predator, already dead while waiting for death, seemingly already dead to avoid death. Such could be the definition of terror; *self-annihilation in the hope of avoiding death*.[1]

Those who terrorise – let's call them 'terrorists' – do not fear death, it is their ally. But the terrorised live in its empire, trying to avoid it by mimicking it. Terror is not fright [*frayeur*], fright strikes like lightning; it 'freezes the blood',[2] expelling the soul, leaving the body listless, quasi-mechanical. 'Frightful' illnesses are known to traditional thought. Spanish speakers say *susto*, the 'physical jolt' that is the air escaping when one is frightened. In Spanish, *asustado*, 'scared', means both someone who is surprised by a barking dog suddenly coming out from behind a hedge, and also someone who has been seized by a spirit, a demon who has slapped them, for instance. These theories are not so far from where we are today. We still use the word *cinglé* [crazy] in French, putting being frightened on the same plane as being whipped by a devil. Someone who is frightened is not terrorised if they retain a lasting mark, or a pathological fear, or a feeling of sadness. They can still use their body, even if it is a body that they control less and less, a body which is sometimes depressed, and sometimes in a rage.

Nor is terror the same as fear, which this time is a real conscious emotion, or on the point of becoming conscious. If it is accompanied by sensations, racing pulse, hot flushes in the upper body, leaving the lower part cold, sometimes trembling. This does not mean that fear isn't still a kind of impacted reasoning that contains the condensed traces of prior experiences. The child who has burnt herself on a hotplate *fears* bringing her hand close again. Fear is 'practical reason' in the proper sense of the term.

So, if terror is neither fear nor fright how can it be defined in its phenomenology? Let me try using a parable. A man walking in a forest turns a corner to find himself suddenly face to face with a tiger. He looks at the animal, which looks at him. This exchange of looks is the precise moment of terror. In that fraction of a second, the man sees what the tiger sees in him: a lump of meat. At the moment he becomes a substance in the eyes of the animal, he is seized with terror. Because the tiger doesn't know who it eats, only what it eats. That is, it has just redefined the man as food. It has defined him as such through its bulging muscles, the strength of its jaws, the way its claws can tear. And the man has no way of getting out of it. He has become, in himself, this lump of meat that the tiger covets. *Terror is characterised by a radical dispossession of being.*

Now we can define the techniques for bringing terror about, or at least their logic; it is about not dealing with human beings any more, but rather with characteristics that one is looking for in them. For instance, you can keep track of sick people, like the Nazis did when they set up their 'Aktion T4' programme, a campaign to systematically assassinate Germans with physical or mental handicaps. Here too, the Nazis only saw in their victims the thing they were feeding off, the physical defect according to the T4 programme, their Judaism or their 'gypsyness' in the application of the 'final solution', their 'slavity' in the search for *Lebensraum*, for the 'living space.' The Nazis were cannibals who liked eating the handicapped, Jews, Gypsies, or Slavs. That's where their terror came from.

Faced with a tiger, I am struck with terror because it has reduced the totality of my being to the few kilos of flesh it will have for its dinner; I am the same for a Nazi, who sees nothing in me but the Judaism he wants to wipe off the face of the Earth.

*A terrorised human is already captive,* because he or she is violently reduced to one single characteristic which is grounds for being devoured, having one's will destroyed, being dispossessed of one's very being. The powerful, the one carrying a weapon, wielding the force necessary to terrorise, can take over a person, use them like a machine or a piece of material. Their singularity is denied, their name rubbed out, their filiation effaced, to the point of turning them into a zombie. They end up being slaves. *Terror is always the starting point of any capture. It is at the source of all slavery.*

It seems that the attacks that have hit France ever since Mohammed Merah's attack in Toulouse in 2012 derive from a concerted strategy to spread terror. It was not a case of killing one or two people, but one of installing a climate of terror with the intention of subjugating France. Not just French Muslims, but starting with them; not just the France of the carefree life and *joie de vivre*, but that too; not just the Jews, or the Christians, or the agnostics, or the atheists, but all of them as well, each category, and each taken individually. Because terror feeds off groups separated from the community, individuals isolated from their group, with their ties loosened. Muslims, hedonists, Jews, Christians, agnostics or atheists – each is a target by virtue of the characteristic that specifies them. Here we can see, covering the widest spectrum, the hand of the organisation that is making sure that no one feels safe.

In this context, where each is a potential target, the weakest try to escape terror by paradoxically aligning themselves with the terrorists. This is why terror often gives birth to terrorists, who will spread terror – terror which will engender terrorists. It is a diabolical mechanism.

How many of those who have joined the ranks of the terrorists to escape terror have ended up committing attacks?

She grew up in a housing estate in the suburbs of Paris. Her mother was from Guadeloupe, and her father was a Russian who had escaped the Soviet Union a few months before the wall came down. She was a love child, coming from an unlikely passionate encounter. Her parents met on the No. 38 bus, coming from the Gare du Nord. He had come off the train, worse for wear, with a week-old beard, thin, gaunt. She took pity on him. She was entranced by his eyes, such a clear light blue, like those husky dogs. He had come straight from Moscow, where he didn't often have the chance to meet women of colour. Or maybe he hadn't looked at them. Now he couldn't take his eyes off her. She was a junior administrator, he claimed he was aristocratic, saying that his grandfather had lands that were stolen by the communists. She took him back to her studio in Aulnay-sous-Bois. He said he was an artist. Painter and poet. No papers. She married him.

Who was this man she shared her life with? To this day she couldn't say. A liar, that much is true! Maybe he wasn't even using his real name. During their ten years of life together, she never once met his parents; he had never introduced her to someone he knew, like a friend or a colleague from work. Not one! He claimed they had all stayed in Russia. But where did he go, when he disappeared for three days straight, sometimes a whole week, with no news? He only worked occasionally, and never spoke about it. It was she who supported the household. One day she had had enough. She threw him out.

She can say that she brought up her daughter alone, without anyone's help, especially the father! And it wasn't easy! The little girl was sweet, but introverted, secretive, and all sorts of problems from the start. Already at the age of three she started to have phobias. She was frightened of everything: men (no surprise with a father like that!), animals as well, cats, dogs, children. When her mother took her for a walk in the street, she gripped her hand like a drowning person grips a plank. She was especially frightened of the night. It took hours to get her to settle, she was so apprehensive about sleeping. If she woke during the night, which was fairly often, she stayed awake until morning. The psychologists who were looking after her ever since pre-school explained that her dreams frightened her; she was probably having nightmares. Maybe. Sometimes she woke with a start, short of breath, heart racing, wild eyes ... And when her mother asked her what was going on, what frightened her so, she replied in sobs: 'A black man . . . a black man . . .'

The psychologists had predicted this would all disappear with puberty. In fact, it went from bad to worse.

The real problems emerged in her seventh year at school, when she was twelve, shortly after her first period. She was withdrawn, her head always lowered, making few connections with others, isolated, she was the laughing stock of the class. They made fun of her, of her respect for authority, of her awkwardness. Her religion was the real butt of jokes. One day, three girls who had made her their scape-goat, had the idea to send her terrifying messages on her mobile: 'You slutty infidel, we are going to cut your throat!' When she got home from school that day, she collapsed onto the sofa and lay there curled up until the next morning, petrified with terror. She was certain that this time she would die. The nasty girls, who had been sending menacing messages to other girls, ended up being caught, and the threats stopped. But the fear of dying became an obsession.

The following year, when she was thirteen, she surprised her mother by getting in with a group of girls from the neighbourhood. They had left school and were aggressively and militantly Islamic. They were not unlike the girls who had threatened her by phone the year before. She went out with them, increasingly failed to turn up at school, started shoplifting in the big stores. At home she picked fights, was contrary, hot-headed and abusive. Yesterday's terrorised little girl had turned into a monster.

One year later, she triumphantly announced to her mother that she had converted to Islam. From now on she insisted on wearing the veil and following to the letter the duties of her new faith. She carried out the five daily prayers, preceded by long ablutions. She would only ingest strictly halal food and gave her mother interminable lists of prohibited items. She swamped her with Islamic teachings and inflammatory diatribes against the Americans, the Zionists, and, of course, the Russians. Her mother wanted to put it down to some 'adolescent crisis', seeing her daughter's conversion as a statement of independence. But when she realised that the child was spending whole nights talking on the phone with a man who was calling her from Syria, and that she intended to go over there to marry him, she ran to the police station to ask the authorities to stop her from leaving the country.

A life story like many others, dozens, no doubt hundreds. It is a story about the troubling development of a fragile young girl, who had suffered unexplained terrors since she was very young, who had grown up putting a lid on her phobic defences. The violent acts of aggression she had suffered at school at the start of her adolescence unleashed an extreme state of terror in her. One might think, with a basic psychological reading, that in order to get over this state she had sought refuge 'in the beast's den', getting close to the girls whose violence had earlier terrorised her.[3]

This quick reading of the kind of drama where the victim is progressively transformed into an aggressor leads to a perfect illustration of the terror cycle, that produces terrorists, who spread terror. It is a perfect illustration, too perfect . . .

I dislike this kind of vision, which sets out to describe people only in terms of their failings, while ignoring their capacities and their gifts, gifts that only they are able to realise. This young girl is unusual. Her identity, by virtue of her birth, is insecure. Her infantile fears, where no one could convince her of the permanency of the world, to the point where she couldn't close her eyes, left her, no doubt, with a trembling soul, a soul on the alert. This all seems true to me. But I would still like to understand where she got the strength for her spectacular reversal. Because, even if she resembles others, this story is first and foremost hers: a kid who is sensitive to the movements of the world, to the point of being possessed by them. Despite her terror – perhaps through the very fact of this terror – she makes a counter-phobic summersault, and heads off into the heart of the network, keeping up a telephonic relationship for months with one of the perpetrators, who offered her *initiation through marriage and combat.*

She was Christian until she converted, willingly attending the evangelical church where her mother used to pray, competing with her in the number of devotionals and psalms learnt. And now she is suddenly cast into a network that had succeeded in sending into Syria a number of often very young girls, from fourteen to eighteen years old, making them the wives of jihadists, and sometimes soldiers as well. The world she now faced, she – this fragile, fearful, trembling girl – immersed her into the heart of the battle, where the movement of ideas coincided with that of history.

What happened was that beyond her fear she perceived the political reason for her recruitment. Here was a Christian with a Russian father. The act of plucking her from the heart of the West and converting her to a combative Islam, would be brandished, she knew, like a trophy. It was not just about her, her personal destiny, it was a way of reinforcing 'the cause'. She would be transformed into a weapon of war. The story of her journey, held up as exemplary, would become a small area held in enemy territory. She could be exhibited, brandished like a flag. Because if the daughters of the West are engaged in 'jihadism', how could it not begin to doubt its options, what it calls its 'values'[4]?

The strategy of capturing the children of the enemy recalls what the Ottoman empire carried out in the fourteenth and eighteenth centuries – perhaps it is a direct inspiration, by the way. There are some very keen historians among the leaders of the Islamic State.

The Ottoman empire organised a particularly sophisticated way of recruiting for its elite groups they called Janissaries.[5] This elite corps was made up of Christian children kidnapped in the outlying areas of the empire. These young enemy souls, snatched from their source, were destined to become Islam's spearhead. The eighteenth-century Turks had a disconcerting euphemism for this capture, *devşirme*, 'collecting', in other words the *harvesting of enemy souls*. The best Christian children (adolescent Greeks, Bulgarians, Serbians, Russians, Ukrainians, Georgians or Armenians) were kidnapped then 'Turkified' and Islamicised before going through military training and being enrolled in the Janissary ranks.

In this way the Turks 'produced' militiamen of unfailing fidelity. Because they were separated, from a young age, from any attachment that might tie them to the past, they only recognised the authority of the monarch. Here we can see that the Ottoman empire understood that the loss of attachment necessarily produces fanatical fidelity.

The Janissaries were a double-edged sword. They deprived the Christian populations under Ottoman dominion of their elites and built up a mystical troupe with an iron discipline, particularly well trained in the art of war.

This strategy of capturing enemy souls only to turn them against their progenitors preceded by several centuries the jihadi wave. Before this, it had reappeared in the constitution of battalions of child soldiers recruited among the defeated nations around the world: Africa (Rwanda, Congo, Angola, Sierra Leone), also South America and the Middle East. It is this same strategy that is expressed by the frenetic proselytising of Islamic groups who launch their siren songs across the beguiling Web towards children with errant souls.

And we can understand why the capture of a 'Christian soul', the essence of the enemy, had a special value in their eyes. The fact is that they staked everything on it! The head of the network telephoned the young girl himself for hours every night, swathing her in religious words that mixed mysticism and sexuality. He was relieved every day, every evening, by a cohort of 'sisters', who swamped her with advice, kept pace with her every thought, by telephone, by SMS, dozens of times a day.

At twelve, the young girl was undoubtedly shaken by her first experience with terror that upset an already fragile balance, yet I am convinced that afterwards she perceived the political strength of the strategy put in place to capture her. And this strategy fascinated her.

A wandering soul turned into the object of a complex strategy for capture, most certainly, but who became conscious of, and even enthusiastic about, the idea of taking part in a general disruption of values. Is she just a prey, and therefore a victim? Was she possessed, in the strong sense of the word, by the forces and powers that drive the jihadists? Was she seduced by the cynical enormity of the destruction project? In the 'construction' of this young radicalised girl, what was the part played by her own earlier, complex psychology and what was the role of a real, genuinely 'revolutionary', political engagement?

Psychiatrists, psychologists and social workers are not trained to take into account such political forces and their part in the construction and evolution of the person. *If it is indispensable, in the clinical work with radicalised or converted young people, to proceed to a detailed analysis of their individual psychological make-up, it is no doubt even more important to be conscious of what is at stake politically, and its emotional and intellectual impact, and, above all, the deliberate strategies put in place to seduce them.* The clinical professional must, as always, help them, stay with them and care for them, but also – and this is new for him or her – combat a 'soul capturing' network that deliberately makes use of efficient methods for influencing and, one hardly need add, media and real financial support.

*Unpicking the influence on a person of such a network means identifying, first of all, the actual strategies and being capable of 'dismantling' them, that is, restoring the theory behind them.*

Terror should never be highlighted publicly. For terror, it must be known, is communicative. Faced with a terrorised person, one is oneself terrorised, without even knowing why. Nor is sharing the emotion any way to 'treat' terror. Journalistic explanations and political statements that thoughtlessly and endlessly paraphrase the emotion end up being accomplices of the terrorist action and contribute to spreading it around.

Furthermore, the concept of 'trauma', by accentuating the weakness of the victims, and erasing their revolt, by prohibiting the expression of their desire for revenge, paralyses contagiously any future victims. The word 'trauma' should be banished from any analysis of jihadi phenomena.

A description of the suffering of the victims is not a good way to respond to terror strategies. The only acceptable response, that both corresponds to our moral needs and our desire to be effective, is *intelligence on terror strategies*. To oppose *the strength of the tiger*, we can only deploy the *skills of the hunter*, who, having learnt all he can about the tiger's rationality, has no fear when going up against it.

Nor should we forget a virtue that is often overlooked in cases of psycho-social treatment: courage! It is impossible to respond to subjection strategies without making use of one's own valour.

# 8

# *Abandoned Children are Political Beings*

Ah, so it all came true. It's so clear now.
O light, let me look at you one final time,
a man who stands revealed as cursed by birth,
cursed by my own family, and cursed
by murder where I should not kill.

Sophocles, *Oedipus Rex*

She came from a family of Franco-Italian aristocrats from the Jura. She was opposed to the dictates of her father, a military man who wanted to regiment his family as if they were in the barracks. As soon as she became legally adult, she headed off for adventures in Afghanistan, the Himalayas, South America . . . Twenty years later, in Miami, the day before returning to France, she ended up finding love. He had been a colonel in the Cuban army and had fled the purges and embezzlements to join the diaspora. He was rough and ready, certainly he had learnt a thing or two from what life had thrown at him. She still had all her adolescent romanticism. They got married. For ten years they tried to have a child. After the medical centre had declared both of them sterile, they then found their application for adoption refused. True, he was sixty-five at the time and she was fifty. Not admitting defeat, they made a secret trip to Haiti, where, in a little village near Jacmel, they 'adopted' twins in an orphanage run by nuns. They then returned to France with their two boys. One of them later said: 'They *bought* us like you buy a pair of boots or a pair of gloves.'

Today, the adoptive parents are both dead, from illnesses, leaving the two kids, then at the age of seven. Despite being educated in the schools of the Republic, they have always known that the core of their being resides over on a Caribbean island, planted under a mango tree in a mountain village. These strangers coming from so far away found themselves one day, at the age of seventeen, the inheritors of this grand aristocratic family, owners of considerable resources in a provincial capital.

One of the twins, who thought of himself as the older because he was born before his brother, was always level-headed, ever since he was a child. He went into a technical college to train as an electrician. The other more sensitive brother had an artistic soul, with his heart set against authority, and was wandering around from the age of fifteen. He goes on long walks around town. Crosses the bridges, perches on the parapets, sits there for hours at a time to watch the birds pass by. He is a pickpocket, dope peddler, sometime burglar. The detentions and reprimands stack up. One day, he 'switched sides' as his tutor said. He who had grown up Catholic and been a choir boy for a long time – now he was a convert to Islam and ready for war. He attends

Salafist prayer groups, buries himself in the study of
fire-arms, and dreams about going to fight in Syria. But
doodling with a pen in the judge's chambers the man he
is constantly drawing is not a pious Muslim, nor even
some mujahidin armed to the teeth, nor a preacher in
the Mosul mosque . . . No, it is the Lider Máximo, with
his military beret, full beard and permanent cigar: Fidel
Castro.

This story sounds very old, almost mythic. But I actually did know this kid of seventeen, who walked on
balcony railings to check he wasn't frightened of heights
– it is a story that reminds me that adoption produces,
as if in its essence, political beings.

They are in play as soon as they are born, things to
be captured and rejected, children who have been driven
out of their families by death, poverty or madness. One
day, as if driven by some internal mechanism, they find
themselves the centre of group attention. These hybrid
beings often create religions; they are the points of origin
from which the myth comes down to us. This is the case
of Moses, you will recall, who was separated from his
parents (Amram and Yocheved), his tribe (the Levi) and
his people (the Hebrews) to be brought up by the daughter of the Egyptian Pharaoh. It is also the case of Jesus,
who is unable to think of himself as the child of his
parents; whose mother Mary had not been approached
by her husband, who had emerged from her womb leaving her a virgin. It is obviously the case of the Prophet
Mohammed, the son of ʿAbdallāh ibn ʿAbd al-Muṭṭalib
and Āminah. His father died before he was born. His
paternal grandfather put him in the care of a family of
Bedouins where he grew up deep in the desert, far from
his mother. One day his foster brother ran to tell the

adoptive parents that Mohammed had been taken aside by two men dressed in white. They supposedly lay him on the ground, opened his chest and reached in with their hands. Later we learn that these two men were angels who had taken the child's heart out to purify it. But the woman who had suckled him, and her husband, knew nothing of this. The Bedouins feared for the life of the child and hurried to take him back to his mother. Three days later, she died. Then it was his paternal grandfather, ʿAbd al-Muṭṭalib, who took him in, but two years later it was his turn to die, but not before handing him over to his uncle who brought him up like one of his own.

It is perhaps in the case of Mohammed that the obligation for adoption is the most demanding, as if there is an incompatibility between being a foundation figure and simply being the son of one's parents.

There is one more of these foundation figures who is particularly famous among psychologists. Of course, I'm talking about Oedipus, whose story has been distorted through constant rehashing.

You will recall that Sophocles' tragedy, *Oedipus Rex*, is based on the abandonment of Oedipus as an infant, immediately after his birth, exposed on Mt Cithaeron.[1] Then he was saved by the shepherd, and eventually adopted by Polybus and Merope, king and queen of the city of Corinth, who brought him up as their own. Then, twenty years later he meets his biological father, Laius, on the crossroad to Delphi, doesn't know who he is, has an argument and kills him. And when he meets his mother Jocasta, the Queen of Thebes, he doesn't know who she is either, and marries her in the ignorance that he has committed, one after the other, parricide and incest. The tension of the tragedy lies precisely in the fact that the spectators know what Oedipus ignores; that he is the perpetrator of the crimes defiling the city that he now reigns over. He then searches for the guilty party in order to purify the city.

But doubt begins to insinuate itself into Oedipus' mind. We sense that he is not far from uncovering the truth. He asks himself if he could have married his own mother. It is at this point that Jocasta utters these famous, often discussed, lines:

> For it hath already been the lot of many men in dreams to think themselves partners of their mother's bed.

Yet Jocasta's statement is mistaken, or at least it could do with some rephrasing, situating it more in time and space. 'In Greece, yes . . . many men, in the Greece of ancient times, think of themselves as partners of their mother's bed . . .' Because 'Oedipus' dreams' are very rare in today's France. In forty-five years of clinical practice, I have only been told such a dream twice. So, we would have to reformulate Jocasta's sentence thus: 'Often ancient Greeks dreamed of intercourse with their mothers . . .' because, unlike us, their culture included the myth of Oedipus.[2]

Reading the interpretation of ancient dreams makes one realise that they are actually deeply imbricated with Greek culture and its socio-political world. The meaning is obvious for ancient Greeks watching a representation of *Oedipus Rex*: the tragedy is about the instinctive attachment that Greeks have to their homeland; they go back to it whatever happens. Oedipus sleeps with his mother, like any Greek would at the end of life when they take to the bosom of the earth, Greece, as a final resting place. And yet Freud postulated, in 1897, that if this play had such an impact on the audience, it wasn't because it played out any local Greek tradition, but the unconscious desires of the child – any male child! – to marry his mother and kill his father. Ever since, psychoanalysts have repeated the same interpretation *ad nauseam*. Nevertheless, they have missed a more trivial psychological reality, as easy to observe as it is common. When a child meets a parent, a mother or father, after a long separation, years later; when he or she suddenly has to feel a strong familiarity with this adult, yet only sees a stranger in them, then a real mental cataclysm jolts them. How are they supposed to choose between the information provided by what they understand, and their spontaneous emotions? The woman who is presenting herself as the mother of the child, who should be the closest person, having spent nine months in her womb, is neither known nor recognised. The somewhat artificial way this mother tries to be convincing disconcerts the child, whose own feelings don't correspond with what has just been learnt. Try as he or she might, the child's mother remains as foreign as a passer-by. Such is the storm battering the child, leaving him or her speechless. The adult, father or mother, is equally in turmoil, suddenly being confronted by this child who they know is so close yet feels like a stranger. Often the child will attempt to get closer in a pretend kind of way; often the parent will come up with all sorts of exaggerated proofs of love, thinking that the quantity will overcome the time gap.

My clinical career has given me many opportunities to meet such real Oedipi – dozens, for sure! The children of migrants left back home, with a grandmother, uncle or aunt, while the parents tried their luck in Europe. When they meet up again with their parents, often a dozen years later, maybe more, one is witness to real tragedies, which might be less theatrical than Oedipus', but can be just as terrible in their effects. The acting out is often violent, with the father as much as the mother; more often there is delinquent or drug-related wayward-ness. But sexual actings-out are rarer, however, and mostly with the father and daughter. Only once did I encounter a case where a family reunion played out with mother–son sex. With time, we come to understand that violence, acting out, sexual excesses, are a way of short-circuiting time, lighting a fire in order to forget the cold, creating an immediate intimacy in the very place where estrangement had created a void of meaning.

My colleagues and I at the Georges Devereux Centre call this configuration the 'Oedipus syndrome', in opposition to the highly celebrated yet non-existent 'Oedipus complex'.

Having converted to a radical Islamic sect, he went off to be a jihadist, somewhere between Syria and Jordan – 'in the Sham country' he told her on the telephone. But, after the telephone calls had stopped for four months, the brutal, terrible news came through: her son was dead. He had supposedly been executed by Bashar al-Assad's soldiers. Unless it was Daesh, as he was getting ready to desert and go back to France ... She learnt this on the telephone from a random who said he was a 'brother'. She didn't believe him. She still doesn't believe him! She is hoping, she wants to keep hoping ... He got away, he is in hiding somewhere, Turkey, Greece or somewhere. She mounted a campaign at the Quai des Orfèvres and the Quai d'Orsay,[3] to try to get news, but no one was of any help. Ever since the cursed day that the death of her son was announced, she has been in the same state, obsessed . . .

She carries herself in that majestic way that African women have, with an enveloping peaceful presence, a taste for thoughtful conversation, with well-chosen words, as if chiselled in the mouth before uttered. She was born in the south of Benin in a village near Allada, of an (Ashanti) Ghanaian father and a Fon mother from Benin. She is conscious that such alliances between people of distant ethnicities is not recommended. The families are so different; their languages, the customs . . . all this can create misunderstandings, disagreements. That is what happened in fact. They separated after two years together. The father went home, way over to the other side of Togo, and she stayed with her mother in Benin, where she had grown up. Strangely, the mother never remarried and had no more children. Sometimes she used to say, half-joking, that it was her daughter's fault because she had 'closed' her, put a padlock on after she left the womb.

As soon as she was weaned, when she was about two, her mother left her with her own mother to go to work in Cotonou. She saw her intermittently, when she came back to the village to visit the relatives. This mother – what can one say? Well, in a word, not good mother material! As for her father, she saw him much later, on the occasion of her marriage. Which, by the way, he was behind, having 'sold' her to one of his friends. She should never have accepted this marriage. It was the start of all her troubles.

So, at age sixteen she leaves her grandmother's house to live with this husband she scarcely knows in Accra, in Ghana. He was certainly much older than her, but he was a businessman. He had painted the villa in glowing colours, the servants, the cars, everything a woman might want! Once she got there she was quickly disenchanted. This was a brutally violent man. He shut her up, beat her, humiliated her, forced her to have sex. She might be living in a villa, but she was treated worse than a domestic. A slave, that is what she had become! She wanted to leave; she wanted to die. When her son was still an infant, she threw herself from the first-floor window in despair. Both legs broken. Three years later, after the birth of her second child she drank a whole bottle of bleach. By some miracle, she survived. She stayed eight years with this man, her husband. For all these years, she only wanted the same thing every day: to disappear, flee, die, be rescued. When she mentioned divorce, he threatened to kill her. He made it clear that, if by some chance she did get away, she would never see her children again.

She was advised by an older relative, taking stock of her physical condition. He said her husband would be the death of her one day. He told her to give up everything, clothes, things, children, and take to her heels. Leave, leave quickly, as far away as possible, anywhere.

And we find her on the road, barefoot, wandering from one church to another, begging a mouthful of *akassa*, the fermented corn pasta sprinkled with a bit of fish sauce. As she would say herself, she was a 'good-looking young woman'. That is how she ended up getting a passage to France. Once there, with the help of distant relatives, she set herself up in the Paris region and never stopped trying to get her children back. During those years, her whole being was focused on that goal.

After ten years of separation, she got them back. Her son didn't recognise her; his own mother! At first he called her 'Madame'. 'But I'm your mummy!' she would retort. He was sixteen, a good-looking boy, tall, thin, elegant. And intelligent as well! After the baccalaureate, at eighteen, he tried the first year at the Sorbonne, then converted to Islam. When he was a child in Benin, he was Catholic, like her – and actually very Catholic, a real little devotee! He was a choir boy, spending all day with the priests. When he joined his mother in France, he was always dreaming about mission work, never missing a chance for a pilgrimage to Chartres or Lourdes.

So, what happened? What bug did he catch, or rather, what devil got into his head? The following year, he went to a madrassa in Egypt, to learn Arabic and study the Koran. On his return, he told his mother about his decision to migrate to a 'truly Muslim' country, where he could live the life of the faithful in harmony with the world around him. In the meantime, he had succeeded in converting his sister, whom he convinced to marry a young man, a second-generation Portuguese who had recently converted to the Salafist sect. She had made '*hijra*, in keeping with the Prophet's migration from Mecca to Medina, but her 'migration' was not as far, since she had joined an Islamic community in the Gers region.

After his mother had remarried, fate had started smiling upon him. With the husband, they were making a respectable living importing African artefacts. But her children had converted to fundamentalist Islam, and she became 'physically and mentally' sick. She was shocked by the reaction of the institutions she went to looking for help. She was so insistent that the police chief ended up showing her the door, 'Your son is an adult, Madame, he has the right to choose his religion!' This was, of course, true, but the police officer didn't realise that this was not a matter of choosing a religion; that it was deeper, much more serious. She couldn't believe that her son had been able to take the path, on his own, from Salafism to armed combat. There were others behind all this; some guru, lieutenants, followers . . .

Once the conversion was in place, the house was a war zone. She had to hide her own cult objects like her missal and statue of the Virgin. When her son saw them, he would explode, 'Idolatry! It is forbidden to believe in statues . . .' And her daughter was even worse. She spent up to two hours in the bathroom doing her ablutions. She checked the provenance of all the food, scrutinising the labels, comparing them to a list of illicit products. Conversation with these children after their conversion became impossible. Everything she said or did was *haram*, sinful. As a Catholic she was treated as an infidel, a *koufar*, or she had become a '*Shaitan*', a devil. Not wanting to lose contact with them, she even accompanied them to the mosque. But questions were not allowed. One day her son prayed on her head. He performed a *roqya*, an Islamic exorcism, wanting to drive out the devil that according to him was resident inside her. Being opposed to the true faith of Islam could only, of course, be an act of the devil.

When she saw her daughter in the full burqa for the first time, it was as though someone had 'planted a knife in her back'. So she went to the children's court to meet a magistrate and other advisers. Her daughter, being a minor, was given a placement by the ASE (social assistance for children) in a foster home. When, today, she looks back over those years of conflict, she is appalled. All the talk, dozens of convocations, interviews, interrogations ... and the result? Nothing! Her daughter is now veiled from head to toe, secluded in some sect in the south-west of France, and her son ... her son is perhaps dead. That's the result!

So, that is how it goes with the 'Oedipus syndrome', which could be described as the impossibility of re-establishing a link that has been dissolved by the absence of a common history. Conversion is precisely one possible resolution of such a syndrome, since it provides reasons for a rupture, and motives for anger. 'If I don't recognise her, this, my so-called mother, then it is because we don't share the same faith ...'

The upshot of this 'Oedipus syndrome' is that this woman's two children have become strangers. She was Catholic; they've become Muslim. While she felt attached, in her bones, to her roots in Benin and Ghana, her children have found another homeland for themselves, Saudi Arabia, the birthplace of the Prophet, where the boy dreamed of going to study religion, and '*hijra* places in France, like the one where her daughter moved in order to live out fully her passion for Islam. Thus the strangeness they felt at the time the family got back together made sense afterwards in the radical heterogeneity of their faith. Now they were really strangers. More than strangers: antagonists.

These aren't unusual situations. Many migrants encounter the same problems. The strangeness of a parent who has been absent too long, the cultural estrangement from ancestors, create a sort of semantic void, especially if there is nothing in the environment to guide the young person searching for answers, especially since no one in this secular land gives any credit to rituals from another age.

*For the young person that no one has guided towards a meeting with ancestors, the solution is then fleeing forwards into a double break: 'Neither Ashanti nor Fon, neither French nor Beninian, nor Ghanaian – a stranger, certainly, but not a stranger from the past, a stranger from the future: a 'real' Muslim, in other words an extreme Muslim.*

'Wandering souls' are really children generated over three generations. First, there are the grandparents breaking with strong ancestral traditions, the complex rituals, the esoteric initiations that stretch over a whole life. Those families in the south of Benin or in Ghana who, over time, have become Catholic, Protestant, evangelical Christian or Muslim, do not neglect the traditional ceremonies: name days, symbolic transmission of heritage and, especially, funerals. But in this family, the grandparents' generation had already neglected the rites, forgotten the devotion due to the ancestors, and deserted the village. The mother, for her part, had only known her parents' Catholicism since her childhood, and she still respected it with a calm faith, far from the excesses of the charismatic or evangelical churches.

So, first break with the grandparents' generation. One might think – as she did, and the village elders even more – that the grandchildren's rupture sanctioned that of the grandparents. The former had abandoned the ancestral cults for Catholicism; the latter abandoned Catholicism for fundamental Islam.

One doesn't break with the ancestors with impunity. They demand their rites, otherwise – the elders would hammer it home – they will spread misfortune and illness among their descendants. Once, when she went back to Benin for the holidays, she went to question a diviner, a sort of priest of ancestral traditions. He threw the *Fa*[4] prayer beads several times (eight half-shells from kola nuts), while uttering formulae in the ancient tongue that she didn't understand. And then he spoke. He told her that the behaviour of the children was a consequence of the abandonment of the rites.

What about the boy's disappearance? For the old man in the village, the verdict was unambiguous. First the ancestors warned, then they punished. Her son was dead. One man, finally, told her the truth.

The old diviner specialising in *Fa*, a traditional geomancy of inordinate complexity, had in this way tried to find a solution for the woman's problems. His proposals might seem anachronistic: come back to the village, keep it alive, put money into restoring and carrying out the ancestral rites, burying the elders, the grand funerals of earlier times, affiliation with family deities ... But, unlike the cohorts of social workers and therapists she had consulted in France, he had immediately pinpointed the genuine questions to do with identity and belonging: '*Who am I?*' '*What group do I belong to?*' He didn't shilly-shally; there was no mincing of words. These questions are matters of life and death.

And he drew from his contribution a blindingly obvious conclusion: against a jihadist ideology that advocates an off-the-shelf identity, it is essential to reconnect with ancestral identity. Reconnect with ancestral identity? Easier said than done, you may think. What is required for such work? Knowledge, of course, that's the easy part; a certain humility also, so as not to hesitate, when meeting with the young people and their family, to ask for the help of the old people in their world, grandparents, elders in the home village, who can tell stories and explain things. But that is not enough. The work of the (ethnopsychiatric) clinician will consist of bringing together ancient knowledges, dramatising them, demonstrating their modernity, culminating in the narration of today's story through the prism of those forgotten thoughts.

# 9

# *The Foreignness of Migrant Children*

I hate travelling and explorers.

Claude Lévi-Strauss, *Tristes Tropiques*, 1955

It took me a long time to realise I was an immigrant. Today, people say 'migrant', perhaps because, if we take the grammar as a clue, the 'immigrant' reaches a destination, while the 'migrant' pursues his or her ineluctable destiny to migrate again and migrate always ... This time, language is right: there are fewer and fewer immigrants and more and more migrants.

I knew, of course, that I was born in Egypt. Every year I remembered, when school went back; we had to fill in those little forms for each teacher: 'Born on ... in ...' 'in: Cairo'. That didn't sound right! 'District: ...' 'District: Egypt'! That sounded even worse! It was a little shameful to stand out like that, a shame that was slowly transformed into a consciousness of one's own difference. *The art of migration consists in trying to convert shame into pride*. I haven't got there yet.

Like most kids who have migrated, I most remember leaving. That moment, on the wharf of the port of Alexandria, after the humiliating body searches, and the confiscation of all cash and jewellery, anything that could be sold . . . that moment when we made our way slowly up the gangway. I wasn't very old; I was nine. I turned around and looked back, between the adults' coats, at this country that was breaking to pieces. I told myself there are moments one should hold in memory, interrupting their fluidity. I was surprised not to feel any particular emotion during this scene, yet I perceived the exceptional gravity, the weight of the threats to my family and myself. I should have been terrified, also sad; I should at least have cried. Deep inside I was stone cold. It seems to me I have consecrated my life to clarifying the strangeness of this moment.

Children are often endowed with prescience. No doubt they have not quite lost that fine perception of atmospheric changes that other primates enjoy, these anxious populations on the alert. I think that if migrant children register with such precision the instant of the break, it is because they have an intuition about misfortunes to come. In my consultations, I have often invited children to tell me about this instant that marks a before and an after, this instant that keeps expanding, until it lasts for a century. Some say it is when the plane took off, others the moment they got into the taxi, lots remember waking up in the plane, after dozing off, and their terrified glance onto a transformed world. For me it was the gangway of the boat. I am forever living these few wooden metres, at the place where I had this sudden desire to go back, a February afternoon in 1957. A few hours later the sun was setting over the prow and Egypt disappeared at the stern.

When you emigrate, you see over and over this passage across an invisible line whose crossing transforms you. At school, in hospital, at work . . . Every time you are asked to spell your name. Every time a law is thrown at you that brooks no exception; when you are blamed for not being like the others. Not being like the others . . .? Ah, you will find out later that no other is really 'like the others'. It's about something else, some essential quality that will come to integrate itself in a person's nature. Migrants ought to be warned: 'Beyond this limit, your *being-in-the-world* will no longer be valid.'

Emigrating is always a case of losing certitude about the world and its reliability, and the matching of word to thing. It is also an exceptional occasion to break with attachments that one thought inalienable, or at least to loosen the halter. Some migrants change their name; even more cut some years off their age. Too good an opportunity to miss, no doubt. But it is a more serious matter than gaining petty advantages. The feeling of identity, I mean the sensation (the illusion?) that one is identical to oneself, that a same self existed yesterday and will still be there tomorrow; this sensation is diluted. I think we can claim from this that migration creates the potential for boldness, but also for despair.[1]

A couple in their early fifties. He is a big, athletic, rather handsome man. She is a little rotund, hair covered with a coloured scarf, a face like a happy moon. They are both Tunisian from the Sousse region in the south. He comes from a little agricultural village, she from a well-to-do neighbourhood in town. They are related, distant cousins. The marriage was first arranged, then became a love-match, or the other way around, cousins who loved each other and ended up getting married. They give the impression of being satisfied being together. He speaks French very badly, while she only has a few words. Yet they arrived a long time ago, in his case about thirty years, she ten years later as a newlywed. He worked hard and ended up buying his own corner grocery store. They were able to buy themselves a house in the southern suburbs, where they brought up their two children. The older, a lovely young woman of about twenty, is enrolled in second-year law at university. It is with the second that they had problems.

At seventeen, he was put under provisional remand within the framework of an order concerning 'association with criminals concerned with a terrorist organisation'. The previous year, in the company of two friends, both over eighteen, he tried to get to Syria for the first time. Stopped at the airport, his passport was confiscated and his parents called in front of the judge, who passed down an injunction on his leaving the country. Six months later, he managed to get out anyway. Spotted on boarding, he was arrested when the plane landed in Turkey. The father claims that the police let him board so they could throw him in jail afterwards.

The parents were heard on several occasions by the police and the judge. They said their piece and were given information on their son's behaviour. It can't be said they were completely surprised because they admitted that they had already been concerned about their son for three years. But, even today, they have kept their confidence in him, convinced that he is going through a bad period.

As for the main issue, they don't understand. What got into him? He was a boy with such a sweet disposition, affectionate with his family, friendly towards strangers. He was good at school and his teachers had a good opinion of him. So, what happened to turn him into a fanatic, a potential assassin? Well of course, if someone goes after him, if he is provoked, then he can end up getting angry . . . it is true he can't stand anyone speaking frivolously about the Muslim religion, or any jokes at the expense of the name of the Prophet. Then he can go into a rage, even get violent. It seems there is a chasm between this son who is immersed in a frenzied kind of modernity, and his parents, who after decades in France have never left Tunisia.

What kinds of relations do these parents have with their children? What language do they speak together? The older girl scarcely speaks any Arabic, maybe she refuses to speak it. As for the boy, if he understands it correctly, he always replies in French. It is true that once they bought the house, they didn't go home every year like they used to. It is from this point that the children seem to have become distanced from the tradition. Culture is often forgotten; it needs to be cultivated! Without that, it disperses; whole swathes of it disappear. The girl is interested in her studies. As for the boy, he is flying so high . . . Two parents locked into a faraway world; two children who have each chosen forms of modernity that can be found in the West.

This family resembles many migrant families. They left Tunisia, sacrificing a country they obviously knew well from their childhood to gain some of the wealth of the world – first the father, then the mother. They certainly hoped not to change their very being, only their environment, try their luck elsewhere, earn their fair share in life. In fact, they scarcely changed, not even learning the language of their host country, or very little of it. Their universe was always down south, in the country they had left. This was the country with which they had daily contact, she with her friends, and both, at a distance, via cable TV which helped them stay in contact with Tunisian news, with their family, or via Skype or Facebook, where they can admire the photos of their nephews, nieces and cousins. Even their life in France remained Tunisian, integrated in the immigrant community. On the other hand, their children who were born in France and educated in public schools, are genuine little French people, modern, conscientious, studious. They communicate with their parents in the usual ways in migrant families. It is often the case that the parents speak the language of origin and their children reply in French. Arabic, if it is not lost, remains for the latter a passive language, including for the boy who has a deep working knowledge of the Koran. '*They understand*', says the mother; '*they don't speak it.*'

We should not neglect *this return of the language* in 'conversions' ('re-conversions') of the 'second generation' of migrants – even if strictly speaking it is not a matter of the same language, the language of the Koran being quite removed from the spoken language. The radicalised young come back to an origin anyway, perhaps further in the past, no doubt semi-imaginary, an origin they can brandish in the parents' faces, accusing them of being deficient, not only in 'Frenchness', but also in 'Arabness', in 'Islamicity.' Having recourse to origins in this way is not fake. It would be wrong to accuse them of not knowing the traditions, having, for instance, a superficial knowledge of the Koran – the origin, as I noted above, is not fixed in the past. It is a matrix on the basis of which a future can be forged.

Even when the situation is not as acute as the one I have just described, the children of migrants end up being strangers to their parents. Often, the parents have tried, in an instinctive fashion, to preserve the original identity, and they are experts in it despite everything, while their children are acquiring a new expertise that is indispensable in the world of the hosts. It is the children who read the official letters, from the health and social services, tax department, the school. They, too, regularly fill in the forms and draft replies to letters of injunction. In certain aspects of daily life, the children become, in a way, the parents of their parents, informing them, guiding them, tricking them sometimes, taking their place. This paradoxical, unstable equilibrium generates tensions, irritations and feelings of isolation, and lasts as long as the environment is calm, as long as there is no litigation with the police, the school, the law or the administration, or no conflict within the family. Problems often arise at the end of adolescence when decisions are being made about romances or life-choices. If the parents have tried to retain the original identity, then they now have to ask themselves why, since they have not succeeded in transmitting it. The day has to come when they look at their children and see only strangers. *The children of migrants do not suffer a deficit, but an excess of integration* – an integration that has taken them too far away from the source. Well, everyone knows that! Educators, teachers, social workers, see it every day. What happens to the worlds migrants have lost?

That, by the way, is what the father said. He thought of his son as just like him. Muslim of course, but not too much, not excessively. He thought he had fitted in, despite everything, seeking social approval, as most Tunisians do, especially those from the South. So why did he rise up against the world around him? As soon as he says this, he backtracks, he wants to start afresh, make it ordinary . . . Everything they say about his son, this is just the judges exaggerating everything . . . But he seems distraught . . .

My heart takes a leap. I feel he doesn't understand his own child.

What I don't like about migration, deep down, is precisely the fact it separated me from my parents. Yet we did live together. In Cairo we had tranquil times and moments of war and violence. We battled through hard times in Rome, lived like the working class in Paris and its suburbs. My parents seemed to watch over me. I made a good show of being their child, both conforming and opposing. But today I can say that all that was made up. I felt other; I had the sense they were somewhere else. We were separated on that gangway on the boat, that cold and sunny afternoon in the port of Alexandria. Something broke there, something impalpable that I cannot find the word for . . . the feeling of being a link in a long chain, going back from child to parents, parents to grandparents. Maybe one could say: a rosary of souls.

I sometimes think that this separation was caused by the loss of our dead. Our ancestors are all buried over there since time immemorial, as many on my father's side as my mother's, in the Bassatine cemetery in Cairo. This cemetery, which was granted to the community by the Sultan Ahmad ibn Tulun in the 9th century, is nothing but ruins today. I doubt I could find my family there. At times of fury against the Jews, the Egyptians desecrated the tombs, broke the steles, carried away stones to erect shacks on the terraces of old buildings. I wonder how they would react when they find Hebrew inscriptions on the stones holding up their huts. Probably with fear!

Just like me, the children of migrants are a long way from their dead. Perhaps their troubles will be a reminder of how much the dead are indispensable to life. I know that it was political forces that we had no control over that threw us out of Egypt. As a child, I felt the vibrations, the walls shaking, the crowds screaming and brandishing truncheons and machetes. When I became an adult I read, travelled, looked and asked questions. Egypt used to be plural and multi-lingual; now it has become almost exclusively Arab and Muslim. It was this political movement, that you could call the homogenisation of the people, an irruption rising from its guts, that expelled us far away. There was no more room for difference. Egypt vomited us up.

Migration has a political motive most of the time. It is made of political events, so the children of migrants are above all political beings. It is for this reason that they are particularly sensitive. Today both my parents are dead, buried in the cemetery at Pantin. I miss them! I already missed them when they were alive.

# 10
# *Generations*

In a society that has abolished every kind of adventure the
only adventure that remains is to abolish that society.

Raoul Vaneigem, 1967[1]

It all started with a string of events that has been repeated
so often since the 1960s, all over the planet, that it could
almost be seen as ordinary. A father, a mother and four
children, thrown onto the path of exile by the political upheavals in a country. It is a Jewish family, you
might say 'traditionalist', but in an old-fashioned way,
sustained by a simple, profound faith without ostenta-
tion. They had always lived in Algeria, but were forced
by a series of pogroms to leave that country. First, they
emigrated to Israel.

The oldest was quite a young man at the time, and
experienced the kind of rootlessness often found among
immigrant children. He was unsure of himself, a failure
at school, attracted by marginality and negativity; he
ended up leaving the family home. He took off on the
road with a young Sephardic Jewish girl, like him a

recent arrival in Israel. They lived on their wits, slept in bus stations, feeding themselves with a bit of shoplifting. A child was born of these adventures, a little girl, under the sign of contingency and precarity. The social services placed the baby, more or less from birth, in the care of her paternal grandmother in a commuter town near the Lebanese border. The child arrived poorly cared for, malnourished, dirty, distressed, unable to make eyecontact. A bad start in life!

Afterwards, not being able to adapt to the rough conditions in the country, the family emigrated once again, this time to France. At the time the kid was nine. They could be thought of as 'coming home', since they were French nationals, without ever having been in France. But from the Jewish point of view, this migration was a failure. Because if in Hebrew one says *'alya* ('ascent') for emigration towards *the country,* which is called the 'land' (*eretz*), then they say the opposite *yerida* ('descent') for leaving it. So this family tumbled into France. And yet the grandparents and each of the children eventually managed to make a good life for themselves, including the father of the little girl, once he got back from his wanderings. But there was a left-over, like a transaction cost, this first girl, born by chance at a difficult time. Her mother, who stayed in Israel, forgot about her. Her father, once he remarried, wasn't interested in her either, wishing perhaps to forget the wayward nights of his youth.

So, in France the kid is once more put in her grandmother's care, with whom she had, since birth, forged an unusually intense relationship. Forever an unweaned baby, no doubt because she had been denied a point of departure; she was also unusually precocious, custodian of the family's core, having grown up between two dreams, two ancestral incarnations: Israel and France. Is this the reason she constantly worried her family? The grandmother's other grandchildren, born in France, seemed to have no issues.

What can we think about her childhood in Israel, between the earlier generation obsessed with images of Algerian happiness, and the subsequent one, that of her parents, who having missed out on the fulfilment of the myth, must settle for perpetual temporariness?

What can we say about her hesitation between two languages, Hebrew in her first years, drowning in exile, and the French of the estates where she grew up in France? She has no idea! She is a little bundle of nerves, her speech fuses, then profuses, words collide; sometimes she makes up neologisms at the crossroads of language. One can feel her oscillating between the temptation to melt into motherly arms and a basic revolt against existence itself.

And when, as an adolescent, it was her turn to spend her nights outside, roaming with gangs, and when the acts of delinquency get frequent enough for the children's magistrate to hand down a decision to put her into care, it is a disaster both for her and her grandmother. Sure, bring her back into line, but separation – never!

The loss of structure suffered by her parents and grandparents first when they were ejected from Algeria with no hope of return, then a second time when they abandoned the myth by leaving Israel, added to the sketchiness of her own filiation turned this young girl, almost an orphan, into a 'wandering soul', easy prey for the buccaneers of souls. Should one be surprised that she ended up being the object of captures of all sorts?

No one wants her, yet all claim her. Social workers intervene, then out of home care. She runs away, a new placement, runs away again, foster family, more running away ... violent reactions ... The authorities, war-weary, recognising the stupidity of the placements, end up giving the young girl back to her grandmother. The directives are raining down, from the courts, the social workers, on the family, the grandmother, who is incriminated in endless reports; the interested parties don't always know what is in these reports, or can't grasp what it means, except for the accusations.

'Who does this child belong to?' I can't answer outside of negations: *not to her parents,* who rejected her as soon as she was born; *not to her grandparents,* who love her like someone from outside the family, a child who has been temporarily put in their care; *not to the care centres or institutions either,* who set up a whole string of 'admissions.' But who, then?

Now suddenly there is talk of kidnapping. The grandmother: tiny, stocky, dynamic, voluble, eyes darting about, watching doors and windows. She is in fear! She has just been told that her granddaughter, now just eighteen and a half, has taken off with an Islamic network and is about to – she fears – leave for Syria.

This is not an imaginary danger. The kid has been seduced by a Salafist Muslim, a man of about thirty. Since her childhood she has been waiting for a new departure. He has been dazzling her with conversation, marriage, a new life in an Islamic country. When he is absent, he delegates 'sisters' to take her in hand, remind her what is forbidden, control her existence, warn her about attempts to deflect her from her new faith. She already thinks she is Muslim. She rejects anyone who tries to reason with her, except for her grandmother who is going crazy with worry. She would so like to reassure her.

The question that possesses the young girl is manifestly psychological, but it is also political. She may not be fully aware of this dimension, but she feels its effects to the extent that it impacts on the environment and above all on her family. She comes from a Jewish community that has been in the Maghreb for centuries – perhaps millennia[2] – suddenly obliged to leave at the beginning of the 1960s. Who are they? Maghrebian like the others, but of Jewish confession? Descendants of ancient Jewish emigrants? That is sometimes what the Jews from Djerba in Tunisia claim. Berbers who converted to Judaism in ancient times? That is the story the Jews from the Atlas Mountains tell. Her family no doubt has connections, as most do, in all three categories. Are they from there, from the Maghreb? Are they still foreign after two thousand years? Eternal foreigners, in essence?[3] If so, what kind of foreigners? Not colonists, for sure! They were humble folk. But definitely others, *strangers within*. These questions that were never asked in their country of origin came to the surface with their exile. When they got to an Israel they thought of as the homeland – homeland of the heart and the faith – they couldn't settle down, they were obliged to emigrate once again. In France they carried on as best they could, but didn't really integrate. They were undermined by each shock of anti-Semitism. They become fearful easily, anxious and hypersensitive, porous when it comes to the kinds of movements of crowds of which they were once victims.

And here is their child, their granddaughter, taking sides with the very people responsible for their expulsion

Generations

from their native land. They know very well they are not identical, but similar in their eyes: fanatical Muslims. Those who incriminate Jews, accusing them of being the source of their misery. Those who take revenge on Jews for the suffering under colonisation. They were able to understand, if not accept, their own banishment. They could see that the young nation was building on new foundations, breaking with the West. But why them? There was nothing Western about them; they had been Maghrebians[4] for centuries. A little francophone, no doubt, but above all they were Arabic speakers and as patriotic as the Muslim population. It is not so much that they misunderstood the tide of history; they just refused to think about it.

They can't ignore the link between the conversion of their kid to radical Islam and their own past. It seems obvious to them that the young girl has incorporated this history, digesting it to the point of embodying its contorted caricature. Assessing the effects arising out of her conversion, one has to consider whether she is doing it in opposition, defying and provoking them, or if she 'radically' tried to resolve the problem they were bogged down in – the enormous, irreparable loss of their ancestral Maghreb. Is she their negative side or their accomplishment, revealing to them what they can't manage to think through: that the past is never past?[5] Or worse, that the past could constitute a matrix for the future?

A singular story if ever there was one, this child of no one, embodying the emotions of a lost world in the intimacy of her contradictions. This is where she is also *of her time*, like the children of Muslim migrants from the Maghreb or Middle East, or those from sub-Saharan

Africa, South-East Asia or elsewhere. A generation that announces it has nothing to do with the preceding one, yet is its chemical precipitation. Radical thought is a mass phenomenon, but it is also the adventure of a generation.[6] At the age when young people used to be initiated – say between thirteen and twenty-five years – this generation wants to demonstrate to the preceding one that they are no longer in phase with the world as it is progressing (that, in other words, the old have nothing to teach the new), and that they are going to draw strength at the place where opposition is least compromised. Hence it is *non-humanist, non-republican, non-pacifist*, and aligns itself with that total ideology which has captured it. So this ideology is at the same time a religion, an oppositional way of life and a political engagement in tune with history, feeding the news, every day, overturning existing worlds. In addition, it pilots an international political activity: the project to reestablish a Muslim caliphate on a planetary scale,[7] yesterday in Yemen or the Sudan, the day before in Afghanistan, today in Iraq, Syria, the Sinai, tomorrow, who knows where . . .

Clearly only a very small minority of adolescents living in France take steps towards radicalisation, but the ideological wave they are carried on infiltrated their environment, their 'neighbourhoods', a long time ago. The burgeoning 'social mass' behind this ideology is much more significant because it is placed as the negative of the ambient liberalism.

This generation irresistibly reminds us of the one that took part in the events of May '68 – mine! Like its predecessor, it calls for a radical break with accepted thinking; like it, it references major international issues.

Finally, like the first, it isn't satisfied by simply criticising ideas or offering new ones. It turns the tables, challenging the previous generation's conception of the world.

It would not be surprising to find cases of Islamic conversion among children of participants from the May '68 generation – children who one day present their parents with the contorted image of the very thing they held in contempt.

Another young eighteen-year-old girl. A quite different life story, just as complex as the above one. While the first was born under the sign of precarity, the second had been long waited for. Her mother was an intellectual who really wanted a child, but was in fear of maternity. Her father didn't have time to think about it. He was an enterprising man, fighting for humanist causes, taking his wife off on missions as a development expert in Africa, the Maghreb, or the Middle East. Each time she found something to do, teaching here, journalism there. Their youthful years went by. At thirty they started wondering, at thirty-five the panic began to set in. When was the child going to arrive? Examinations, treatments, keeping on trying ... Still nothing! Yet according to the clinic there was no impediment. As a last resort, during a visit to her parents in Basque country, the wife paid a visit to Lourdes to pray to the Virgin – neither of them was a believer. Before you could say 'boo', the pregnancy arrived, when they had given up hope.

The childbirth was terrible, and the gynaecologist made it clear to the parents that they should give up the idea of a second pregnancy. As soon as she arrived, the infant was a treasure. Her parents decided to bring her up like no other child had been before, researching the most modern methods. They taught her to read at three; at six she could recite whole Victor Hugo poems. The father was so flabbergasted by the intellectual capacities of his child that he started her on sciences and history. She could give lectures at thirteen. Without a doubt a super-gifted child, pampered, overinvested. But what weighed on her like an absolute obligation were her parents' choices. Whatever they did, exactly as they did, she could do better!

He came from a small town in the Loiret; she from a Basque farming family. They are meritocrats; they got where they were through relentless study; the republican ethos is deeply rooted. They met in university lecture halls. They have been reading and studying ever since. They both dream of getting doctorates, but everyday obligations have put that off until later. Maybe at retirement . . .

At fifteen, their daughter shut herself in her room, was contrary, flew into rages over nothing. What happened for her behaviour to change so much? She used to hang onto her mother's apron strings, and now she was lying to her, criticising her clothes, her friends, her ideas. Of course, adolescence . . . But also something happened that she only told her parents about two years later. She was fourteen, already maturing, with a grace that drew glances. In the course of a visit to her paternal grandfather's, she was allowed her first glass of wine, and a neighbour, an adult of some thirty years, started to fondle her. For this young girl – intellectually precocious but affectively dependent – this event let loose a genuine cataclysm. Overnight she lost the confidence she had in adults.

At seventeen, the year of her baccalaureate, during yet another argument with her mother, with accusations and tears, she suddenly announced that she was going to leave home and live with a young man, from Mali, a Salafist Muslim, and that she had already converted to Islam. Until this moment the parents had suspected nothing. The next day she was gone. Her father tried hard to mediate, thinking he would be able to bring her back to reason, and back home. She received him in her boyfriend's apartment dressed in an ample black djellaba, only to break the news that she was five months pregnant, and that he had better get used to the idea that this was her new life.

Her parents belonged to a later generation than 1968, nourished with the theoretical choices and morals brought about by that cultural upheaval. Coming from modest backgrounds, they both liberated themselves, by their own volition, from the weight of French pre-war traditions. They decided to rise in the world together, but more on a moral scale than on a social one. They chose freedom of thought, and became resistant to any religious dogmatism. They were fierce advocates for women's liberation; women should be at least as well educated as their husbands, engaged like them in tertiary education and have real jobs. They battle against injustices and inequalities and are instinctively resistant to anti-Semitism and racism. They are passionate about development, taking on all the struggles of outcasts, social rejects, the 'damned of the earth.'

And here in their own house they see the spectre of everything they rejected emerging; the ideas, the retrogressive behaviour that had earlier been thrown in history's rubbish bin. They wanted a liberated daughter, and she falls pregnant at eighteen, making further study problematical. They wanted her to be an intellectual, an academic or researcher, and they find her with simplistic manuals that regulate the daily life of a good Muslim woman. They dreamed of her realising the exceptional intellectual capacities that they had cultivated in her all through her youth, and now they feel she is stuck in an old world ideology. And that is how they ended up alone, the two of them, the father with his disappointment and the mother with her outrage.

No one can predict the destiny of these two young girls, the Maghrebian Jew tempted to leave for Syria, and the intellectuals' daughter shut up in the studio of a Malian Salafist in the northern suburbs. Both are fascinated by the radical choice of a generation that has nothing in common with the preceding one. Will they slide more and more into Islamic radicalism, take up arms, or slowly come back to society as it is?

I can't stop myself from reminiscing about my twenties. 1968 was much more than a conviction; it was a faith with a magic word, a mantra: 'Revolution' . . . I haven't forgotten. My friends were there, from Picardie, from the south-west, or maybe the sons of a few generations of Parisian workers. They had their parents on their back, who were capable of identifying our ideology. They had known communism and syndicalism; it all resonated for them . . . Nothing like that at my place. My parents sometimes called me an 'anarchist', but it was by way of a joke, as if it was fun for them to say the word. They didn't have the common base, the things that go without saying, the innuendoes, the depth of local history. They were immigrants. I saw in their eyes a reproach marked with impotence, as if they wanted to warn me: 'Don't get mixed up with that; it isn't our business!' Deep down, without being entirely conscious of it, I thought so too. These events in 1968 could only become 'our business' (the business of Jews banished from Egypt)[8] on condition of being 'everyone's business'. We wanted to replace a universalism that we found narrow, with a more extensive planetary universalism. This was the ideal, I think, that was being called 'revolution'.

I turned twenty in 1968. They called us *'enragés'* or 'leftist'; we defined ourselves as anarchists, 'situationists' or *'mao-spontex'*. These were little differences, which we blew up through refusal, we weren't going to be like this. We weren't *'révisos'*, the social-traitors of the communist party; certainly not Stalinists – we called them 'stalopes'.[9] I can't say I was a 'Marxist' even though I spent weeks slaving over the *Contribution to the Critique of Political Economy*. I definitely had no interest in the economy. I was a dedicated Freudian, totally imbued in psychoanalytic thought, at least in the books, a long way from the couches, the institutional apparatuses, the baronies and the apostolic successions that characterised real psychoanalysis, as I found out later.

Today most of the talk is about the leaders: Dany Cohn-Bendit, Alain Krivine, Roland Castro, Alain Geismar, Benny Lévy . . . they forget that there were up to a million people in the streets, fighting and digging up paving stones. There weren't a million leaders. I was part of the infantry. I was a *fantassin* – a word coming from the Italian *fantaccino* – a 'child' in other words. My misunderstanding of the real political objectives allowed me to move through the events as if they were Saturnalian nights.

It isn't possible to find any statistics, but I am convinced that the great majority of students who took part in this movement were newcomers: children from modest backgrounds, the first in their family to do higher education, children of migrants from the countryside or simply migrants from elsewhere, like us. Us, the 'immigrants from North Africa' as they said at the time. Close to us also were the children of yesterday's immigrants, from Poland, Italy or Spain . . . We were not inheritors![10] Our knowledge of it was imperfect, we only knew a little of the earlier world. When we marched yelling, 'We are all German Jews', in order to oppose the expulsion of Daniel Cohn-Bendit, we also wanted to say, precisely, that we were not inheritors. That, just like him, we were foreign to the ordering of that world.

I am not the first to have noticed that a great number of the leaders of the fringe groups of May '68 were the children of exiles, resistants or migrants – many came from Jewish families.[11] It has to be said that in France the young Jews of my generation, those who were about twenty in 1968, found themselves with a double heritage, that of the Shoah – the faces of the dead exercised an absolute pressure on us – '*to metabolise the terror on seeing those emaciated bodies, seeing those blank looks, lost in absence*',[12] and that of the obligation to make a new world in common with those who wanted our relatives dead.

The slippage first happened in language, as is often the case. Before the war, and even through to the 1960s, people avoided saying the word 'Jew'. In official discourse and administrative documents they were still using the term 'Israelite'. An unlikely expression was even invented: 'French of Mosaic confession'. These were euphemisms, of course, whose usage, in fact, kept the word 'Jew' available for anti-Semitic insults. When it made its return to current usage, in the course of the 1970s, the word remained charged with negative connotations. It was then that the younger generations diluted it properly: they accepted the Pariah role that the epithet 'Jew' carried, on the condition that it was identified with all the rejects of the world. By operating a translation of the Jewish singularity (possibly painful) to a universal abstraction of suffering humanity, they reclaimed the ground of avant-garde of the damned of the earth.[13] It was thus that they moved from the unbearable assignation lived during the war to identification with all the pariahs of the world on a grandiose quest. I have to say, my generation has been impregnated with this paradox which allowed it to extract itself from the burden of a weighty identity. Jewish, maybe, but like the Palestinians, like the Africans, the Vietnamese . . .[14]

Coming from the war, seeing all those cadavers lying there, becoming aware of the systematic destruction that his or her people had undergone, a young Jew couldn't, logically speaking, escape the question of revenge.

Vladimir Jankélévich was one of those rare thinkers not to forget it, to give this question a prominence in what he wrote. One remembers the brouhaha that he provoked when he said on television, on an *Apostrophe* episode – and this was in 1980, more than thirty-five years after the Shoah! – that he would never go to Germany, would never quote a German author, would continue to forget the German language, and would never shake hands with a German, even one born after the war.[15]

He carried in his heart the impossibility of forgiveness. This was not, as far as I understand, the expression of a personal emotion. It was an actual philosophical position. In this way Jankélévich delivered a message that was addressed to us, the following generation. Very few of us actually listened.

The question of revenge was clearly present in the youth of 1968, but travestied, hidden beneath political rationalisations. The person who incarnated it in the clearest way was without a doubt Pierre Goldman. Born in 1944, he was twenty-four in 1968. He had a derisive attitude towards the May events: 'They don't realise that their revolution is nothing but a game', he said – a game that he qualified with 'pornographic excitation' and 'collective onanism' . . .

For his own part, he fully took on the issue of revenge: '*I was born a Jew in danger of death. I was never old enough to fight, but could have perished in the Polish crematoria. The children were the first assassinated.*' They wanted to assassinate me; I will take revenge; thus was Goldman's fury – a fury born at the same time as himself, and it seems it never left him. He acted on the 1968 movement in its dying days like a developing agent, bringing its hidden part to the surface. How can you take revenge on an enemy that has evaporated? How can you confront Nazis when they have disappeared? A few years earlier he drafted a constitution for urban guerrillas. His ideas – too extreme, or too advanced – were rejected, including by the radicals. So he went off to fight in South America . . . no doubt to look for the unfindable Nazi, to hunt for an inevitable battle, carry out his revenge.

Goldman's involvement in communist movements

since his childhood, then in an increasingly more extreme radicality, fed off the memory of the Shoah. His models were the heroes of ultimate revenge, the rebels in the Warsaw ghetto, Mordechai Anielewicz, Marek Edelman, or the boldest fighters in FTP-MOI.[16] He gave a veritable cult status to Marcel Rajman, who carried out thirteen attacks on the Nazis in the middle of the Occupation, with grenades, machine guns, pistols. It was Rajman[17] who had succeeded in killing Julius Ritter, who was in charge of the STO [compulsory work] in France. You could say that Goldman continued the fight, at least in thought. He was extremely involved in the same way as Marcel Rajman, following his example. Rajman's life came to a brutal end at the age of twenty one, on 21 February 1944, a few months before Pierre Goldman was born on 22 June 1944. Pierre Goldman, the child, took the place of the dead, Marcel Rajman.

There is no doubt that the generation of 1968 was a radical one, 'enraged' by its disputes with the past, with its political disputes as well, cherishing new projects for society and the world, heads bursting with revolutionary ideas, and hearts alive to a new universality.

This generation of migrants and children of migrants came out of May '68 disappointed, sometimes bearing wounds, with certain knee-jerk thinking, with blind spots hiding a bit of the world from them. Some hit the ground hard. I know some who never got over it. Others – most! – went back to general society more or less successfully, not the society of the 'subjected' – we called them 'sheep' – but of the 'realists', who accepted that they had to give up some ideals, swapping them for a foothold in the world. I must say I was neither with the first nor the second, neither those who did not want to admit that the movement had ended, not those who, having buried it, never stopped mourning it. I have remained a radical, keeping my radicality for my discipline. I wanted to build a psychotherapy based on the pragmatics of migration, in fact. A psychotherapy that makes no pacts with any powers that be, not with the pseudo-biology of pill-peddlers, nor with lecture-hall psychoanalysis.[18]

My generation was just as radical as that of the young people who have converted to jihadist Islam. I waited a long time before I became aware of the impossible revenge that inhabits us, that also leaves us with a feeling of irreality. No, the CRS were not the SS. Of course not![19] But we didn't have any SS handy . . .

We know the past disputes that obsess today's radicals; they are basically ones to do with colonisation; political disputes also, the way they are stacked away in the housing estates of the suburbs, their extreme employment difficulties, the denial of social acceptance. All this is known, of course. Are they conscious of the pernicious strength of impossible revenge? They too have a project for a new society and a unified, universal, world, this time under Islamic law. I increasingly think that the demand for universality is a poison.

The person who most explicitly formulated the end of impossible revenge, describing both ancient disputes and the belief in a new universality, is no doubt Khaled Kelkal, the terrorist responsible for bombing the St Michel RER station in 1995.[20]

Here is what he said to Dietmar Loch, a German sociologist, who was asking him about integration in 1992:

I am neither Arab, nor French, nor Muslim. [. . .] If now the French became Muslim, they will be the same as me. We will bow down before God. No more races, nothing more, everything dies down, it is unity. [. . .] Now, you go to the mosque, it is full of French. [. . .] You go into the mosque, you are relaxed right away, people shake your hand, you are thought of as a long-term friend. There is no mistrust, none of the prejudices [. . .]. We are brothers even if we don't know each other.[21]

So it is certain that the young people who are involved in jihadist Islam today are not just a part of this generation, they are its spear-head – or at least, they think of themselves as such. In this respect they are not just people who think, in the excitement and the rage, but are also thoughts incarnated in people. They represent – they know! – the historical and geopolitical debates. They come to demand the payment of a bill for which their parents are the creditors. They represent a network of different ideas, and help them rise to the surface by committing acts that break with common sense.

And the result of their actions is that the intangible principles of modern democracy are turned inside out, like a glove. We came out of the war with three prohibitions: *no anti-Semitism, no barbarous murder, no mass ideology.* And now these three monsters are reappearing in an extreme form in these Islamic ideologies, sometimes rampant like in the estates, sometimes carved out and brandished like a sabre when jihadism is carried out.

# Epilogue

... it [writing] will introduce forgetfulness into the soul of those who learn it: they will not practise using their memory because they will put their trust in writing, which is external and depends on signs that belong to others, instead of trying to remember from inside [. . .] Your invention will enable them to hear many things without being properly taught, and they will imagine that they have come to know much while for the most part they will know nothing. And they will be difficult to get along with, since they will merely appear to be wise instead of really being so.

Plato, *Phaedrus*

I had a gut feeling about this book, even now it has my stomach in knots. I spent a lot of time unable to write, as if the material challenged the act of writing itself. The young people I am speaking about here, rootless radicals, question the meaning of existence and remind us of death. When I took to the road with them, exchanging words, 'dialectics' as we used to say, it seemed to be ambushed at every turn, a minefield behind each word. So, to write. But why write? And how?

I had difficulty meeting them. They have the fragile narcissism of the rejected, agreeing to come out of the shadows, but finding themselves in the glare of the spotlight. And I was only able to invite them to what I knew how to do, the slow knitting together of a provisional meaning that inscribes one step in the world at a time, waiting for the next. I think they appreciated our meetings. For my part, I learnt so much from the exchange. It is that, what I learnt – not what they taught me, but how they made me think – that's what was worth passing on, in my opinion.

When they bite the bullet and decide to convert, plunging body and soul into their new faith (Salafist Islam is about daily mastery of the body, its hygiene and nourishment, and a ceaseless surveillance of the soul), these young people are no longer content with meaning, they are on the hunt for signs. A given event in the world, far or near, is a sign, a divine message.[1] They interrogate it, question it among themselves, seek out their masters' answers. What's more, they know that they themselves have become signs. Signs of the times, the way a generation is talking, as I explained, but also signs of movement, announcing a cataclysm on the way. This is why disorder is something achieved, signalling the proximity of the upheaval; disequilibrium equals confirmation; strangeness equals evidence. And these words, that we hear from time to time, give us goosebumps, but they certainly are an indication of the reversal of values, as attributed to Hassan el-Banna, the founder of the Muslim Brotherhood: 'Death on the path to God is our ultimate wish.' It is no use trying to plead with them to be reasonable, to try to *understand*, rather they have to be *read*, like the signs that they have the presentiment of having themselves become. Understanding the meaning, or reading the signs, two opposite methods whose origins we can trace back.

There are books that transmit information, that are written to be told about, set out, explained, informed about, and others that contain signs. The latter can be read or scanned; sometimes it is enough to open them randomly, close the eyes and put the finger on a page. They are interrogated like the oracle, as if we were asking them to show us a sign. Here the reader is not the only actor, the book is too. The young Senegalese girl, with whom I had long discussion about the veil, nurtures a fascination for the Koran. Of course, it is still also a book, this Koran that in Arabic is sometimes called *el kitab*, 'the book', *par excellence*. She came to learn Arabic later in life, and it was a revelation. This girl, quite young, was born in France and her first language was her parents' Wolof, and her second the French of her school-mates. She marvelled at the perfect beauty of the Arabic writing, its poetry, the philosophical ideas between the lines that emerge during the recitation. I don't know where this intuition for language came from, but it played no small part in her enthusiasm for Islam. It was there, at this crossroad of sound and meaning, that we were able to have a long discussion.

They speak of the 'invention of writing' with the understanding that there was a time in the history of civilisations when it was absent. But there have never been people without writing. The problem is not put the right way: 'Who is writing? and Who is reading?'

. . . that's the right question. There once were – maybe they still exist – peoples where only the gods write. They used to call them 'peoples without writing'. And among other peoples – we, the 'moderns' – people write even more than the gods.

A surprising idea, I must admit, these gods writing for the edification of humans. Voodoo deities in Benin or Togo write into the events of the world, organising their succession with an invisible hand. History, here, is written. One event happening is a message, another is a different one, the order they come in is yet another. So, the questions are infinite. All at once people have installed a writing desk between them and their gods. The diviner – over there they say *baba lawo,* the 'master of the secret', he whose job it is to read – throws his *Fa* rosary (eight palm nut half-shells tied to a cord) onto a dark wooden dish covered with kaolin. Then he 'reads' the signs, whether the half-shells have fallen open or closed, also according to the traces they have left on the white powder base. Here people are 'reading' what the gods write. The system of interpretation, based on the two hundred and fifty-six combinations possible after eight successive throws of the rosary, constitute a kind of alphabet that only diviners know how to decode.[2] At the heart of these peoples, therefore, gods write (in the *Fa* language) and men read. Elsewhere, in Mali, in Dogon country, diviners examine tracks left at night by little pale foxes, when they disturb sticks that have been left with some food between them.[3] Once again, an esoteric alphabet, made up of the position of sticks in the morning, whose signs are combined infinitely in order to read the writing of the gods. Elsewhere, on the Ivory Coast, it is mice whose movements in boxes that have two levels are examined; in the Congo, kinds of tarantula that move among the twigs . . .

Who is writing in these polytheistic worlds? It isn't the nuts, the foxes, the mice or the spiders. They are just auxiliary; pens animated by the gods. And every time it falls to men to decipher, to 'read'. But our gods, in the monotheistic traditions, write just as much, at least that is what is told to us in the sacred texts.

In Hebrew, Leviticus, the third book of the Pentateuch, is called Vayikra, because it begins with just that word, *vayikra*, which is in general translated by 'he called': '*God called Moses and said to him* . . .' (Leviticus 1: 1). That's how the text begins. But the meaning of *vayikra* can be disputed. Does it really mean 'to call', or rather 'to read'? Because the verb 'to read', *likro*, conjugates to *yikra* in the third person singular. So, to say that God called Moses, that is 'chose him', 'designated him', 'assigned him', the text literally has 'God *read* Moses',[4] . . . Meaning what? That God reads a kind of writing, drafted by him, and this godly reading animates the world? It is a plausible interpretation, because Moses comes running, and presents himself at the 'meeting tent' to learn about his assignation. And what does God want? Only that Moses write . . . what God is dictating to him, in fact, the Torah, the written law. But until that moment, the text tells us, Moses does not know how to write.

In the story of the Muslim revelation, we see a very similar scene. Mohammed is staying up in the cool of the night covered in a cloak. A creature of light gives him a silken scarf and orders him: 'Read!' . . . On the material a word is written in golden lettering: *Ikra* . . . which in Arabic[5] also means: 'Read!' And yes, it is the same word as in Hebrew ... 'But I don't know how to read', Mohammed protests. And the angel Djibril (Gabriel), the one with all the revelations, shakes him, almost suffocates him: 'Read!', he orders once again.

Did Mohammed 'read' the Koran, or did he write it? Qur'an, the Koran, is a word from the same root, the word in Arabic that can be rendered as 'reading' or, in the usual translation, 'recitation.' Perhaps one can also add, should one follow the Hebraic connotations, the third meaning of 'call'.[6]

Thus the call of God, or the reading of his text, or even its recitation, according to the translation, has to have an interpretation since writing is here *both meaning and sign*. The ambiguity is just as present in Christian thought. For example, the Pentecostal disorders, the disorder caused by the 'tongues of fire'. Saint Paul was so aware of this that he wanted to put some order into the numerous godly calls falling from heaven. In the fifteenth chapter of his First Epistle to the Corinthians, he recognised that the call can be manifested as *echolalia*, that is, involuntary speech coming to the faithful in unknown tongues, or even in prophesies. But he knew that these irruptions of intemperate words can be the source of cacophony, and in this way put the Church in danger. That is why he warns the faithful: '*If any speak in a tongue, let there be only two or at most three, and each in turn ...*'

On this occasion, if God manifests himself in the form of discourse and not signs, there still has to be an initiated reader: This is why Paul adds: '*... and let someone interpret*' (First Epistle to the Corinthians 14: 27).

I have seen Paul's recommendation applied to the letter in evangelical churches in Africa. I saw one of the faithful prophesising 'in tongues' – a language that sounded to me like an incomprehensible gibberish. I saw the one that they call the 'reporter' run toward him, a notebook in his hand.[7] After that, the pastor, without doubt the most competent in the congregation, 'translated' (interpreted) the words gathered by the 'reporter'.

Paul was right. When God expresses himself, one has to have an interpreter, a 'reader' who makes the divine message clear again. Because 'reading' does not always mean 'read a book'. And Paul goes on: '. . . *if there is no one to interpret, let each of them keep silent in church and speak to himself and to God*' (14: 28).

I had to go through these theological preliminaries in order to be more explicit about the status of this type of discourse, whose expression, traversing the speaker, is both that of absolute knowledge and innocent speech – in a word, *prophetic*. Silence is preferable to no interpreter! I was left confused by certain words that the young radicalised people said to me, reminding me of the omnipresence of their god in the world, warning me of the imminence of the apocalypse, drawing my attention to the cunning of false gods, the devil, demons, the harmfulness of 'idols'. I am convinced one has to 'read' their speech, and even more their behaviour, as signs. So, when it is a matter of telling their story, coming to terms with it, each word should be thought through, weighed, each idea pored over, explored, pressed to the limit. That is what I have tried to do here.

Trying to write about the effect of this speech is a bit like taking dictation from the gods, from God or other beings, according to one's convictions. To do that I have absolutely had to give them space, in other words time to spread out and find room for resonance, to seek solitude for the body and silence of the soul.

I found this solitude at the time that insomniacs toss and turn. I was only able to write at night, jumping if I heard the rustling of the wing of an owl or the tiny footfalls of mice in the loft. I had no need to look for silence. It covers this countryside, at the top of a hill, in a locality with about twenty inhabitants, where the only sound is that of the wind in the leaves, that is melded with the hiss of absence. I finished at first light, when the chaffinch would sing her first prayers.

I like this passage from the Koran that recognises, it seems to me, the necessary collaboration between humans and non-humans to arrive at the clarity of speech: '*Say: If men and jinn should combine together to bring the like of this Quran, they could not bring the like of it, though some of them were aiders of others*' (Surat 17, verse 88).

If it goes without saying that the word of God is of an incomparable perfection and beauty, connecting with beings perhaps makes it possible to get closer to such perfection.

I also wrote this book to bear witness to the complexity of generational replacement in a time where displaying one's differences isn't recommended. Today I am certain that the radicality of the young people I met comes from the growing difficulty that our societies have in integrating difference – not the 'similar' that we keep hearing about, but the other, the really other, radically other. If we persist in sharing a world with the 'similar', we have to expect endless conflict.

The radicalised youth speak endlessly of God, they make him speak to them deep down, obliging us to respond, to demonstrate that there are other gods, ours, and those of other peoples. As they keep drawing attention to this obvious war of the gods, the beneficial effect of their words is to make us come to think more about a world where gods, multiple as they are, like peoples, will agree to live together in peace.

I mostly came across young people who were born here, but with distant, wandering souls. I learned, with them, that they matured by being reconnected to their core. I tried to help them, every time I could, to have more consistency, more depth. On the other hand, I will say nothing about what I did in our confidential meetings. I will say nothing about my strategies, my techniques, my tricks, my successes and failures . . . and my delight also, as well as my pain, sometimes. I will hold my tongue! I do not know who is going to read me . . .

# Notes

**Prologue**

1 The Nazis ordered the rounding up of Jews on 16 and 17 July 1942. They were sequestered in the 'Vél' d'Hiv' (*Vélodrome d'hiver*, 'Winter Velodrome'), a bicycle stadium that used to be near Bir-Hakeim metro station – trans.

2 The *Cité Radieuse* was one of Le Corbusier's urban forms – trans.

3 Reference here to Marshal Pétain – trans.

4 Karl Marx, 'Introduction' to 'Contribution to the Critique of Hegel's Philosophy of Right', in *Karl Marx: Early Writings*, 43–59, T. B. Bottomore, ed. and trans. NY: McGraw Hill, p. 52.

5 These fires have been smouldering for some time. In 1994 I wrote, 'God, give us the strength to regain our humanity before we are annihilated by our suburbs.' Tobie Nathan, *L'Influence qui guérit*, Paris: Odile Jacob, 1994, p. 193.

6 Tobie Nathan, *Nous ne sommes pas seuls au monde: Les enjeux de l'ethnopsychiatrie*, Paris: Points Essais, 2015.

7 David Thomson has covered some significant ground on this question in, *Les Français jihadistes*, Paris: Les Arènes, 2014; and *Les Revenants: Ils étaient partis faire le jihad, ils sont de retour en France.* Paris: Le Seuil/Les Jours, 2016.

## 1 Secularity and the War of the Gods

1 Published as 'Wissenschaft als Beruf', Gesammlte Aufsaetze zur Wissenschaftslehre (Tubingen, 1922), pp. 524–55. Originally a speech at Munich University, 1918, published in 1919 by Duncker & Humboldt, Munich. From H. H. Gerth and C. Wright Mills (trans. and ed.), from *Max Weber: Essays in Sociology*, pp. 129–156, NY: Oxford University Press, 1946.

2 As is often the case in French, Latin gives the common usage and Greek the scholarly one.

3 English readers may be interested that 'secular' comes from L. *saeculum* 'generation, age', used in Christian Latin to mean 'the world' as opposed to the Church – trans.

4 These languages were designated with the pejorative term 'patois' from Old French 'patoyer', 'to talk with the "pattes" [paws], with the hands', 'gesticulate' . . . languages which were therefore not really languages because they had need of signs.

5 *'pays'*, related to 'pagan' – trans.

6 The word refers to a famous episode in the *Fourth Book* where the slave drivers, followers of the Pope, have required a population shown to be anticlerical to extract a fig from the anus of a mule with their teeth.

7 A recent work by Jean Birnbaum (*Un silence*

*religieux. La gauche face au djihadisme,* Paris: Seuil, 2016) underlines what is wrong with the French intelligentsia's obscuring of religious questions.

8 The human sacrifice sequence that grants an increase in the vitality of his god exists in many mythologies, and in the three monotheistic religions: Abraham's sacrifice of Isaac, Jesus as *agnus Dei,* 'lamb of God' sacrificed by his 'father', and finally Ismail by Abraham.

9 I noted one of the origins of this war of the gods in an event that was recorded not in the Bible, but in an old midrashic commentary: Abraham destroying the idols. See Tobie Nathan, *Quand les dieux sont en guerre,* Paris: La Découverte, 2015.

10 Jean-Paul Sartre, *The Devil and the Good Lord,* trans. Kitty Black, NY: Random House, 1960, p. 122.

## 2 The Veil as Membrane

1 We find this same *phrenos* protecting the breath from the impure miasma of the viscera, for example in our word schizophrenia, where it takes on the meaning of 'soul'. Schizo-phrenia, 'split soul', or more precisely, 'dissociated'.

2 There is a first name that derives from this word, *Ma'hjoub* (more often in the feminine, *Ma'hjouba*), that means 'enveloped', 'protected'. Such a person is protected, since birth, without the necessity to have recourse to some amulet. So, the person is 'lucky'. As the French say, so-and-so is 'born head-dressed' [*né coiffé*] – literally with part of the amniotic membrane on the skull – in other words the infant is said to be 'lucky', 'blessed by the gods'.

3 It is useful to discuss the Jewish case. Some passages in the Bible suggest that women were not veiled. Think, for example, of the passage where Abraham passes his wife Sarah off as his sister, fearing that the Pharaoh, in thrall to her beauty, would assassinate the husband and make off with the wife (Genesis 12: 11–15). If the Pharaoh can fall for Sarah's charms immediately, her beauty must not be concealed. However, as we know, orthodox Jewish women have adopted the strangest of veils, the wig. On reflection, the wig is the best way of hiding one's hair without drawing attention to it. Because, in certain passages of the *Talmud*, if a woman is veiled with a cloth it is easy to unveil her. But if it is a wig . . .

## 3 Filiation and Affiliation

1 Cain's eye, the Earth's curse because it was disgusted at having to absorb in its belly the blood of a murder . . . 'Cain's Eye' is certainly a source. See Tobie Nathan, 'L'œil, le poison magique et le talisman. Cause et sens en pratique ethnopsychanalytique', in *Anthropologie et Sociétés*, vol. 17, no. 1–2, 1993, pp. 99–124.

2 Mustafa bin Abd al-Qadir Setmariam Nasar, known as Abu Mus'ab al-Suri, was born in 1958 in Aleppo, Syria, a longtime associate of Bin Laden and Al-Qaeda.

3 See especially the analysis of this intellectual's influence by Gilles Kepel, *Terreur dans l'Hexagone. Genèse du djihad français,* Paris: Gallimard, 2015. For an interpretative biography see Brynjar Lia, *Architect of Global Jihad: The Life of Al-Queda Strategist Abu Mus'ab Al-Suri,* Oxford: Oxford

University Press, 2009, and also the analysis by the Israeli Philipp Holltmann, *Abu Mus'ab Al-Suri's Jihad Concept,* Moshe Dayan Center, 2012.

4 In issue 15 of *Dabiq,* the journal of the Islamic State in English, the target is in fact Christianity, the theme being 'Break the Cross'. In addressing Christians, Daesh explains the uncompromising hate that Islam has for them, for religious reasons, and also for their alliance with secularity. It invites them to mass conversion. In the same issue can be found testimonials of former Christians who have joined the Islamic State: a Finnish woman, a Trinidadian (from the Island of the Trinity! Probably a pun . . .)

5 In fact, being Muslim or Christian is to be repentant in a certain manner. So, we may ask whether one can be a repentant jihadist, repentant of repentance. Could this be possible?

## 4 Conversion and Initiation

1 Alluding to the well-known saying from *Thus Spake Zarathustra,* 'Become what you are.'

2 It is necessary to look at the way the words 'initiated' and 'initiation' are spoken in the languages of the groups practising it. For the most part, initiation is a 'birth'; the uninitiated are new-born, babies, and an 'initiated' is simply a man. Therefore second birth . . . or true birth? See Philippe Laburth-Torla, *Les Seigneurs de la forêt. Essai sur le passé historique, l'organisation sociale et les norms éthiques des anciens Beti du Cameroun,* Paris: L'Harmattan, 2009; and especially Michael Houseman, *Le Rouge est le noir. Essais sur le rituel,* Toulouse: Presses universitaires du Mirail, 2012.

3 See the descriptions of the very complex coming of age initiations in New Guinea, for example by Maurice Godelier, *La Production des grands hommes. Pouvoir et domination masculine chez les Baruya de Nouvelle-Guinée*, Paris: Champs Flammarion, 2009.

4 One has to say that these initiation rites have remained incomprehensible so long as anthropologists described them from the outside. Then some were perhaps a little more adventurous and tried a little harder to reconstitute the situation, instead of armchair theorising, and offered themselves up to the experience. See, for example the celebrated study by Robert Jaulin, *Les Sara du Tchad: La Mort sara. L'ordre de la vie ou la pensée de la mort au Tchad*, Paris: Plon, 1982.

5 Young initiands undergo physical violence (circumcision, scarification, tattoos); long ordeals of suffering (sleep deprivation, obligation to remain naked exposed to intense heat or cold, kept on a strict diet, etc.); degrading abuse (beatings, insults, ridicule, subjection to the initiators' whims, being held in a state of submission and worry); and also absurd abuse (like learning to 'hunt' by going on all fours for hours, or that 'cultivating a field' means drinking an emetic concoction and emptying one's stomach; that 'forging' means getting one's finger smashed by a burning log; that 'fighting' with the main elements of initiation means getting the circumcision wound anointed with a caustic substance ...). These examples are from Michael Houseman, who attempted a global synthesis in this article: 'Éprouver l'initiation', in *Systèmes de pensée en Afrique noire*,

Paris: CNRS, 2008, pp. 7–40. But the main reference is Gregory Bateson's *Naven*, first published in
1936: *Naven: A Survey of the Problems suggested
by a Composite Picture of the Culture of a New
Guinea Tribe drawn from Three Points of View*,
Palo Alto: Stanford University Press, 1958. And see
my own discussion in *L'Influence qui guérit*, Paris:
Odile Jacob, 1994.

6 In Greek philosophy, the word *metanoia* signifies 'a
radical change of one's point of view . . . or existential philosophy'. With Christianity, the meaning is
sometimes inflected towards 'repentance', but most
towards conversion. As for conversion to Judaism,
we know it can only happen after a long appren-
ticeship in study and a maturation of one's desire
to become a Jew. It is perhaps there, in modern
Judaism, that the word conversion acquires its full
meaning as a personal choice that is thought out and
argued for.

7 We elaborate on this idea in Tobie Nathan and
Lucien Hounkpatin, *La Parole de la forêt initiale*,
Paris: Odile Jacob, 1996.

8 See the impressive number in Bertrand Méheust,
*Jésus thaumaturge: Enquête sur l'homme et ses
miracles*, Paris: InterÉditions, 2015.

9 Such is the example of Joppa (Jaffa), a city Peter
converted thanks to a sick person being healed, or
rather, by the resurrection of a dead person: 'In
Joppa there was a disciple named Tabitha . . . she
was always doing good and helping the poor. About
that time, she became sick and died, and her body
was washed and placed in an upstairs room . . .
when the disciples heard that Peter was [there], they

sent two men to him and urged him, "Please come at once!" . . . when he arrived he was taken upstairs to the room. All the widows stood around him, crying and showing him the robes and other clothing that Dorcas [Tabitha's other name] had made while she was still with them. Peter sent them all out of the room; then he got down on his knees and prayed. Turning toward the dead woman, he said, "Tabitha, get up." She opened her eyes, and seeing Peter she sat up. He took her by the hand and helped her to her feet. Then he called for the believers, especially the widows, and presented her to them alive. This became known all over Joppa, and many people believed in the Lord.' Acts of the Apostles 9: 36–42.

10 At the heart of jihadic movements we find most are converts, whether they come from another faith (Christians, Jews, or agnostics) or, most often, from traditional Islam. This is also what David Thomson noted in *Les Français jihadistes*, op. cit. The 'converts' coming from a traditional Muslim family even use the term 'reconversion', as if they had to stress the necessity to go down the path once again, to be basically 're-born'.

11 Georges Devereux, 'L'identité ethnique. Ses bases logiques et ses dysfonctions', in *Ethnopsychanalyse complémentariste*, Paris: Flammarion, 1972. See my comments in my 'philosofiction' essay in *L'Etranger ou le pari de l'autre*, Paris: Autrement, 2014.

12 What language did my ancestors speak among themselves? Did they have one in common? What about two, three, four generations before me?

13 See Tobie Nathan, *Quand les dieux sont en guerre*, op. cit.

## 5 Apocalypse

1 We are the hardy young,/coming to climb to the stars/in a procession of brothers./Let's grasp each trembling hand/knowing how to save our bread/as we build a tomorrow/that sings.

2 On accusations of sorcery brought against children in central Africa, especially in the Congo, see Tobie Nathan, 'Le mystère des enfants sorciers?', *Philosophie Magazine*, n° 63, 2012, pp. 30–6 and to get an idea of how widespread the phenomenon is, see the UNICEF report by Aleksandra Cimpric, *Children accused of Witchcraft: An Anthropological Study of Contemporary Practices in Africa*, UNICEF WCARO, Dakar, April 2010.

3 The Prophet Mohammed located the battle of the end of times in Syria, between 'Amaq and Dabiq. One of the brains behind Daesh, Abu Musab al-Zarqawi, wrote in 2016: 'The spark has been lit here in Iraq and its heat will continue to intensify, God willing, until it burns the Crusader armies in Dabiq.' Daesh took up with this same eschatological rhetoric, spreading it via social media, to the point of naming its press agency Dabiq, as well as its quarterly on-line journal in English. For a general account of this issue, see Jean-Pierre Filiu, *L'Apocalypse dans l'Islam*, Paris: Fayard, 2008.

4 The Yoruba live in Nigeria and the south of Benin. They are both profoundly rooted in their traditional (voodoo) culture, and at the same time open to modernity: commerce, of course, but also industry and high-level scientific research. For a succinct outline of the Yoruba creation myth, see Tobie Nathan and Lucien Hounkpatin, *La Parole de la forêt initiale*, op. cit.

5 Superbly elucidated by Nietzsche: 'Never, in other words, can a being which possesses definite qualities or consists of such be the origin or first principle of things. That which truly is, concludes Anaximander, cannot possess definite characteristics, or it would come-to-be and pass away like all the other things. In order that coming-to-be shall not cease, primal being must be indefinite.' *Philosophy in the Tragic Age of the Greeks,* trans. M. Cowan, Washington DC: Regnery Publishing, p. 47.

**6 Hashish and Assassins**

1 Marx, K. *Introduction to A Contribution to the Critique of Hegel's Philosophy of Right.* Collected Works, v. 3. NY, 1976 [1843].

2 ... with the same connotations as in French, the verb *hash* meaning literally 'stuff'. The adjective, *mahshi,* that derives from it, is used for example for zucchinis or eggplants that are 'stuffed'.

3 On wine and its relationship to Dionysius/Bacchus, see the key article by Michel Bourlet: 'L'orgie sur la montagne', *Nouvelle Revue d'ethnopsychiatrie,* n° 1, 1983, pp. 9–44.

4 European varieties of Datura are known in the countryside under the names of 'devil's snare' or 'witches' weed'.

5 See Peter T. Furst's old but fairly complete study, *Flesh of the Gods: The Ritual use of Hallucinogens,* London: Allen and Unwin, 1972. And more specifically on peyote, the classic by Marino Benzi, *Les Derniers Adorateurs du peyotl: Croyances, coutumes et mythes des Indiens huichol wirarika,* Paris: Gallimard, 1972.

6 See epigraph to this chapter.

7 Georges Devereux developed this kinship between gods and rugs in his own way in a breakthrough text, 'Drogues, dieux, idéologies', Medica, no. 103, 1972, pp. 13–20

8 Dieudonné M'bala M'bala is a French comedian, actor and political activist – trans.

9 See the famous novel by Vladimir Bartol, *Alamut*, trans. Michael Biggins, Seattle: Scala House Press, 2004 [1938], and more recently *Samarkand*, Amin Maalouf trans. Russell Harris. London: Quartet, 1992. And above all, to evaluate the veracity of the legend, see Farhad Daftary, *The Assassin Legends: Myths of the Isma'ilis*, London: I. B. Taurus, 1994.

10 'The idle man has taxed his ingenuity to introduce artificially the supernatural into his life and thought; but, after all and despite the accidental energy of his experiences, he is nothing but the same man magnified, the same number raised to a very high power. He is brought into subjection, but, unhappily for him, it is only through himself; that is to say, by the part of himself which is already dominant. *"He would be angel; he became an animal."* Momentarily very strong, if indeed one can give the name of strength to what is merely excessive sensibility without the control which might moderate or make use of it.' Author's emphasis.

## 7 Terror

1 Georges Devereux developed the same idea in a famous oft-cited article, 'La renonciation à l'identité, défense contre l'anéantissement', *Revue française de psychanalyse*, vol. 31, no. 1, 1967, pp. 101–42.

2 Tracing the most likely etymology, *frayeur* would come from Latin *frigidus*, 'frozen'. For changes in the lexicon of *frayeur* in different languages, see Tobie Nathan and Nathalie Zajde, *Psychothérapie démocratique*, Odile Jacob: Paris, 2012. [But *fright* in English goes back to Germanic roots. – trans.]

3 This could perhaps be described as an instance of 'identification with the aggressor' or 'Stockholm syndrome'. 'Identification with the aggressor' is one of the defence mechanisms listed by Anna Freud in her famous work, *The Ego and the Mechanisms of Defence*, London: Hogarth Press and Institute of Psycho-Analysis (Revised edition, 1968 (UK)). This book was first published in Vienna in 1936, at a time when such mechanisms also had a political implication. There was a great temptation, especially among psychoanalysts, to make pacts with the devil, that is with the Nazis, in order to save the Psychoanalytic Institute of Berlin.

4 See *Dabiq*, no. 15, where testimonials from former Christians are published after they joined up with the Islamic State. The way they are presented is clearly intended to edify: convincing Christians that their destiny is to become Muslims.

5 From the Turkish *Yeniçeri*, meaning 'young (or new) troop'.

## 8 Abandoned Children are Political Beings

1 In ancient Greece, exposure of infants was not an isolated phenomenon. It was the current mode of birth control or resolution of problems of filiation (illegitimate births, for example) and it was the traditional expression of the total power of the pater

familias. See Pierre Brulé, 'L'exposition des enfants en Grèce antique: une forme d'infanticide', *Enfances & Psy*, 3/2009 (n° 44), pp. 19–28.

2 Many illustrations of this can be found in the marvellous *Oneirocritica* (The Interpretation of Dreams) by *Artemidorus Daldianus*, who even had a particular category in his classification of dreams – a category that he in fact called 'Oedipus dreams'. Here are some brief examples:

Therefore, if anyone possesses his mother through face-to-face intercourse, which some also call the 'natural' method, if she is still alive . . . if his father is sick, he will die . . . since the dreamer will take care of his mother both as a son and as a husband. But it is lucky for every craftsman and labourer. For we ordinarily call a person's trade his 'mother'. And what else would having intercourse with her mean if not to be occupied with and earn one's living from one's art? It is also lucky for every demagogue and public figure. For a mother signifies one's native country . . . when he makes love . . . the dreamer will control all the affairs of the city.

And if the dreamer is estranged from his mother, they will become friends again because of the sexual intercourse . . . It also, signifies, therefore, that a son will return from a foreign country to his own land . . . But if his mother is dead . . . what else would intercourse with a dead mother signify to a sick man if not that he will have intercourse with the earth?

It is not good to possess a mother who is looking away from one. For then either the mother herself will look away from the dreamer, or his native land, his trade, or any present undertaking . . .

Possessing one's mother from underneath while she is in the 'rider' position is interpreted by some as signifying death to the dreamer. For a mother is like the earth . . . the earth lies above the dead only and not above the living . . .

. . . however, the worst dream by far is one in which the dreamer practises fellatio with his mother. For this signifies to the dreamer the death of children, the loss of property, and grave illness . . .

3 The Police Headquarters and the Ministry for Europe and Foreign Affairs. – trans.

4 For a precise documentation of *Fa* divination, see especially Bernard Maupoil, *La Géomancie à l'ancienne côte des Esclaves*, Institut d'ethnologie: Paris, 1988 [1943].

### 9 The Foreignness of Migrant Children
1 I have further developed this fluctuation of the feeling of identity among migrants in my *L'Etranger ou le pari de l'autre*, op. cit.

### 10 Generations
1 Raoul Vaneigem, *Traité de savoir-vivre à l'usage des jeunes générations*, Paris: Gallimard, 1967, trans. Donald Nicholson-Smith, *The Revolution of Everyday Life*, Practical Paradise Publications, 1972.

2 In Algeria, Morocco and Tunisia one could together count at least 600,000 Jews, to which can be added 40 or 50,000 Libyan Jews. Some came with the Muslims driven out of Spain in the thirteenth, fourteenth and fifteenth centuries, others were there for much longer, having come with the Romans at the very start of the Christian era.

3 See the work of Georges Bensoussan, putting an end to the rosy pictures of a peaceful cohabitation of Jews and Muslims in the Maghreb, for example: *Les Juifs du monde arabe. La question interdite*, Paris: Odile Jacob, 2017.
4 Words can have an ironic destiny. *Maghreb* means 'occident' in Arabic, 'where the sun sets' and *maghrebi*, 'maghrébin' literally 'occidental'.
5 Paraphrasing the book by Eric Conan and Henry Rousso, *Vichy, un passé qui ne passe pas*, Paris: Fayard, 1994.
6 I mean adventure in two ways: 'a risky or surprising enterprise' and also 'misguidedness'. Recall that Malek Boutih, member of parliament from the Essonne, called the report he tabled in June 2015, *Génération radicale*, wanting to stress that radicality is not assessed by the number of people affected, but by its 'social mass', the prevalence of its ideas among a generation.
7 This is why it is crucial, for social workers and counsellors alike, to think about radicalisation in terms of political strategies. On this topic see the stimulating and well-documented little text by Pierre-jean Luizard, *Le Piège Daech*, Paris: la Découverte, 2015.
8 A Jew from Egypt, no doubt a special one, was in fact the brains behind the Maoist intellectuals from the Ecole Normal Superieur, from the Union of the Marxist-Leninist communist youth and the proletarian Left: Benny Lévy. See Philippe Lardinois, *De Pierre Victor à Benny Lévy. De Mao à Moïse?*, Bruxelles: Éditions Luc Pire, 2008.
9 A rude neologism amalgamating the word for 'slut', *salope* – trans.

10 I allude, of course, to the famous [1964] book by Pierre Bourdieu and Jean-Claude Passeron, *The Inheritors: French Students and Their Relation to Culture*, Chicago: University of Chicago Press, 1979. By the time I got there, this university of 'inheritors' was already on the way out.

11 Yaïr Auron has written a book about this, translated into French under the title, *Les Juifs d'extrême gauche en mai 68*, Paris: Albin Michel, 1998. By the way, ten years earlier, Hervé Hamon and Patrick Rotman had taken up this question several times in their essential work, *Génération*, Paris: Seuil, vol. 1, 1987, and vol. 2, 1988.

12 Nathalie Zajde, 'Guérir le syndrome du rescapé', *Libération*, 29 January 2008. See also, Nathalie Zajde, ed. *Qui sont les enfants cachés? Penser avec les grands témoins*, Paris: Odile Jacob, 2014.

13 This is how a '68 veteran explained it: 'I had to get rid of all that in order to continue to live. Israel was not my problem, nor my battle. I didn't live there. There were Jews over there? Fine . . . In the camps also, there were Jews, all sorts of Jews . . . I had lost my roots and I couldn't find other ones.' Yaïr Auron, *Les Juifs d'extrême gauche en mai 68*, p. 59.

14 Bernard Kouchner is perhaps the most representative of this tendency. He writes: 'When I was in Biafra, in El Salvador, Afghanistan or Vietnam, I always thought that it was a place for a Jew. Jews should be wherever people are suffering. That's what being a Jew means . . .' cited in *Génération*, op. cit.

15 This is how Robert Maggiori remembers it in an article on a new edition of Vladimir Jankélévich's writings (*Libération*, 25 September 2015), a collection

stretching from 1943 to 1983 called *L'Esprit de résistance*, Paris: Albin Michel, 2015.

16 Francs-Tireurs et Partisans-Main-d'Œuvre Immigrée. Units in the French communist resistance during the war – trans.

17 He was arrested by the special brigades on the 16 November 1943, and tried along with 23 FTP-immigrés and given the death sentence. He was shot at Mt. Valerian the 21 February 1944 with 21 members of the Manouchian group.

18 To understand how psychotropic drugs come from pseudo-biology, refer to the work of Philippe Pignarre, especially *Puissance des psychotropes, pouvoir des patients*, Paris: PUF, 1999 and *Les Malheurs des psys*, Paris: La Découverte, 2006.

19 CRS = SS was a May '68 slogan, the CRS being the riot police – trans.

20 Khaled Kelkal: a good pupil in primary school in an estate at Vaulx-en-Velin, then a delinquent tearaway in his high-school years, Islamic radicalisation in prison and then moved on to the terrorist attacks he is known for (assassination of the imam Sahraoui on 11 July 1995, bombing of the St Michel station the 25 July 1995, attack at the Place de l'Etoile 17 August 1995). He was shot and killed by the police on the 29 September 1995, at the age of 24.

21 Interview excerpts from an article in *Libération*, 7 October 1995.

### Epilogue

1 What are sometimes called 'conspiracy theories' are nothing but the visible part of the transformation

from the desire for meaning to possession by the sign.

2 See the account by Bernard Maupoil, *La Géomancie à l'ancienne côte des Esclaves,* op. cit. This book is extraordinarily precise, and so erudite and faithful that the voodoo priests of today treat is as 'Writings'.

3 Marcel Griaule and Germaine Dieterlen, *Le renard pâle,* Paris: Institut d'ethnologie, 1965.

4 In modern Hebrew, the word *kara* means both 'he reads' and 'he calls'.

5 Is there any need to point out that Hebrew and Arabic are related, coming from the same root?

6 In any case, the Koran is sometimes called the *adh-dhikr* (the 'reminder'). The fact is that the word is ambiguous and could be of non-Arabic origin. Some modern Islamic scholars see in the word *qur'an* (the 'Koran'), an adaptation of the Syriac *qeryana*, signifying 'lectionary' (or 'epistolary'), that is, a liturgical work containing passages of sacred texts read on ceremonial occasions. On this point, see Claude Gilliot, 'Le Coran, production littéraire de l'Antiquité tardive ou Mahomet interprète dans le "lectionnaire arabe" de La Mecque', Revue des mondes musulmans et de la Méditerranée [on-line], n° 129, July 2011, http://remmm.revues.org/7054

7 With Lucien Hounkpatin I wrote an account of this very widespread phenomenon for the reception of the word of God, Tobie Nathan and Lucien Hounkpatin, *La Parole de la forêt initiale,* op. cit.